GENDER INEQUALITY

Feminist Theories and Politics

Judith Lorber
City University of New York

Roxbury Publishing Company
Los Angeles, California

Library of Congress Cataloging-in-Publication Data

Gender inequality: feminist theories and politics/Judith Lorber.
　　p. cm.
　　Includes bibliographical references.
　　ISBN 1-891487-02-7
　　1. Sex discrimination against women. 2. Sex role. 3. Women—
　　　Social conditions. 4. Equality. 5. Feminist theory. I. Title.
HQ1237.L67 1998
305.42'01—dc21　　　　　　　　　　　　　　　　　　　97-26297
　　　　　　　　　　　　　　　　　　　　　　　　　　　　CIP

Gender Inequality:
Feminist Theories and Politics

Publisher and Editor: Claude Teweles
Copy Editor: Arlyne Lazerson
Production Editor: Carla Max-Ryan
Assistant Editors: Helen Wallace, Joyce Rappaport
Production Assistant: David Massengill
Typography: Synergistic Data Systems
Cover Design: Marnie Deacon Kenney

Printed on acid-free paper in the United States of America.

This paper meets the standards for recycling of the Environmental Protection Agency.

ISBN: 1-891487-02-7

Roxbury Publishing Company
P.O. Box 491044
Los Angeles, California 90049-9044
Tel: (213) 653-1068 • Fax: (213) 653-4140
E-mail: roxbury@crl.com

In Memory of Zina Segre
May 8, 1933 - April 27, 1997

"Her wounds came from the
same source as her power."
—Adrienne Rich

Contents

Preface

Despite an enormous output of scholarly and popular books and articles, what feminists have actually thought and fought for in the last 35 to 40 years is being forgotten. Popular books criticizing feminism and women's studies have jumbled and caricatured complex ideas and portrayed feminists as man-hating, puritanical "women's libbers." Feminist activism has been coopted to sell Nikes.

What I have tried to do in this account of current feminism is, first, to show that there is a variety of feminist theories, and how the various theories diverge and converge. Second, I describe feminism's significant contributions to redressing gender inequality in order to give credit for its accomplishments, to document on-going political activism, and to indicate the work still to be done.

As my ideas coalesced, I have given talks around the world on the topic, and some of these talks were published. In September 1995, I spoke on "The Variety of Feminisms in the U.S. Women's Movement" at the Non-Governmental Organizations Forum at the United Nations Fourth World Conference on Women, held in Beijing, China. An excerpt was published in the *Status of Women Journal* of the British Columbia Teachers' Federation (Vancouver, Canada, March 1996).

In April 1996, I presented "The Variety of Feminisms and Their Contributions to Gender Equality" at the Eastern Sociological Society Annual Meetings held in Boston. During May and June of 1997, in conjunction with the Marie Jahoda International Visiting Professorship in Feminist Studies at Ruhr University, Bochum, Germany, I gave longer versions of that talk at the Workshop on Feminism and Social Change, and at the University of Bielefeld; Wolfgang Goethe University, Frankfurt; Humboldt University, Berlin; and Carl von Ossietzky University, Oldenburg. That talk has been been published in English by the Universitätsreden BIS (Bibliotheks-und-Information System), CVO University, Oldenburg, and in German in *Feministische Studien,* as "Kontinuitäten, Diskontinuitäten und Konvergenten in Neueren Feministischen Theorium und in Feministischer Politik" ("Continuities, Discontinuities, and Convergences in Recent Feminist Theories and Politics").

Some sections of this text have been adapted from my book *Paradoxes of Gender* (New Haven, CT: Yale University Press, 1994).

The input I got from students and faculty at all these presentations was enormously helpful, as were the comments of the reviewers of the book manuscript. Throughout, the discussions and critique of Maren Carden, Susan Farrell, Eileen Moran, and Barbara Katz Rothman, my multi-feminist writing group, have made my thinking clearer. I particularly thank Susan Farrell for her information on women ethicists and feminist religions.

I also thank Claude Teweles for getting me started on this book and Carla Max-Ryan for her work and patience during its writing and production.

—*Judith Lorber*
New York City

About the Contributors

Edna Acosta-Belén is Distinguished Service Professor of Latin American and Caribbean Studies and Women's Studies, and Director of the Center for Latino, Latin American and Caribbean Studies (CELAC) at the University at Albany, SUNY. She is the founder and co-editor of the *Latino Review of Books*.

Maxine Baca Zinn is Professor of Sociology at Michigan State University, where she is also Senior Research Associate at the Julian Samora Research Institute. Her publications include *Women of Color in U.S. Society* (co-edited with Bonnie Thornton Dill), *Through the Prism of Difference: A Sex and Gender Reader* (co-edited with Pierrette Hondagneu-Sotelo and Michael A. Messner), and *Diversity in Families* (co-edited with D. Stanley Eitzen).

Christine E. Bose is Associate Professor of Sociology, Women's Studies, and Latin American and Caribbean Studies at the University at Albany, SUNY. She was the founding Director of the Institute for Research on Women (IROW).

Hélène Cixous is the Director of the Centre d'Etudes Feminines at Paris VIII University and the author of more than 30 works of political fiction as well as numerous plays and collections of critical work. Her publications in English translation include *The Exile of James Joyce or the Art of Replacement, The Newly Born Women, "Coming to Writing" and Other Essays, Three Steps on the Ladder of Writing, Manna, Hélène Cixous's Reader,* and *Rootprints*.

Nancy J. Chodorow is Professor of Sociology at the University of California, Berkeley, a faculty member of the San Francisco Psychoanalytic Institute, and a psychoanalyst in private practice. She is the author of *The Reproduction of Mothering, Feminism and Psychoanalytic Theory,* and *Femininities, Masculinities, Sexualities: Freud and Beyond.* She is currently working on a book titled *The Power of Feelings: Personal Meaning in Psychoanalysis, Gender and Culture.*

Patricia Hill Collins is Charles Phelps Taft Professor of Sociology in the Department of African-American Studies at the University of Cincinnati. She is the author of *Black Feminist Thought: Knowledge, Consciousness, and the Politics of Empowerment,* which has won many awards, and co-editor of *Race, Class, and Gender: An Anthology* (with Margaret Andersen), which is going into its third edition. *Fighting*

Words: Black Women, Critical Social Theory, and the Search for Justice is scheduled for publication in 1998.

R. W. Connell is Professor of Education at the University of Sydney. He was Professor of Sociology at the University of California, Santa Cruz; Professor of Australian Studies at Harvard University, and Professor of Sociology, Marquarie University, Sydney. He is the author or co-author of 15 books, including *Class Structure in Australian History, Making the Difference, Gender and Power, Schools and Social Justice,* and *Masculinities.* He is a past president of the Sociological Association of Australia and New Zealand.

Bonnie Thornton Dill is Professor of Women's Studies and Affiliate Professor of Sociology at the University of Maryland. Her research focuses on African American women, work, and families. She is currently conducting a research project on coping and survival strategies of low-income single mothers in rural Southern communities.

Cynthia Fuchs Epstein is Distinguished Professor of Sociology at the Graduate Center of the City University of New York. She has been a fellow of the Institute for Advanced Study in the Behavioral Sciences, a Guggenheim Fellow and winner of awards of the American Bar Association and the American Sociological Association. Her books include *Woman's Place: Options and Limits in Professional Careers, Women in Law, Access to Power: Cross National Studies on Women and Elites,* and *Deceptive Distinctions: Sex, Gender and the Social Order.* She is also the author of numerous articles on gender in professions, occupations, and political spheres, and on theoretical and methodological problems in gender research.

Lillian Faderman is Professor at California State University, Fresno. She is the author of *Surpassing the Love of Men: Romantic Friendship and Love Between Women from the Renaissance to the Present* and *Odd Girls and Twilight Lovers: A History of Lesbian Life in Twentieth-Century America,* as well as two books on ethnic minorities.

Roslyn L. Feldberg is a sociologist committed to improving women's conditions of employment. She has written on social and technical changes in clerical work and on comparable worth. Now she is working to improve the conditions of work for nurses from her position as Associate Director in Labor Relations at the Massachusetts Nurses Association.

Jane Flax teaches political theory at Howard University and is a psychotherapist in private practice. Her publications include two books, *Thinking Fragments* and *Disputed Subjects.* A new book, *Hearts* *of Whiteness: The Clarence Thomas Hearings and Contemporary Ameri-can Dilemmas of Race and Gender,* will be published in 1998.

Donna Haraway teaches science studies, feminist theory, and women's studies at the University of California, Santa Cruz. She is the author of *Modest_Witness@Second_Millenium.FemaleMan(c)_Meets_ OncoMouse (TM): Feminism and Technoscience; Primate Visions: Gender, Race and Nature in the World of Modern Science; Simians, Cyborgs, and Women;* and *Crystals, Fabrics, and Fields: Metaphors of Organicism in 20th Century Developmental Biology;* as well as the influential article, "A Cyborg Manifesto: Science, Technology, and Socialist-Feminism in the Late Twentieth Century."

Heidi Hartmann is Director of the Washington-based Institute for Women's Policy Research, a scientific research organization on policy issues of importance to women, which she founded in 1987. An economist, she has co-authored *Unnecessary Losses: Costs to Ameri-cans of the Lack of Family and Medical Leave; Women's Access to Health Insurance; Combining Work and Welfare: An Alternative Anti-Poverty Strategy.* In 1994, she was the recipient of a MacArthur fellowship award. Commonly referred to as the "genius grant," this fellowship was awarded to recognize her pioneering work in the field of women and economics.

Nancy C. M. Hartsock is Professor of Political Science at the University of Washington in Seattle, where she teaches graduate courses on the philosophy of social science and twentieth century Marxism and contemporary feminist theory. She is the author of *Money, Sex, and Power: Toward a Feminist Historical Materialism* and co-editor of *Building Feminist Theory* (with Charlotte Bunch, Jane Flax, Alexa Freeman, and Mary Ellen Mautner). She is currently completing a book titled *Post-Modernism and Political Change: Issues for Feminist Theory.*

Deniz Kandiyoti teaches social science at the London School of Economics. She is the author of *Women in Rural Production Systems* and the editor of *Women, Islam, and the State.* She has been Chair of the Research Committee 32 of the International Sociological Association.

Rosabeth Moss Kanter holds the class of 1960 Chair as Profes-sor of Business Administration at the Harvard Business School. She is the author of 12 books and over 150 articles on organization, man-agement, and social change, most recently, *Frontiers of Management. When Giants Learn to Dance* received the Johnson, Smith & Knisely Award for New Perspectives on Executive Leadership and was trans-lated into 10 languages. *Men and Women of the Corporation* was the winner of the Society for the Study of Social Problems C. Wright Mills Award for the year's best book on social issues.

Thomas Laqueur is Professor of History at the University of California, Berkeley. He is the author of *Making Sex: Body and Gender from the Greeks to Freud* and co-editor of *The Making of the Modern Body* (with Catherine Gallagher). He also writes on the cultural history of death in modern Europe and on memory and commemoration in the twentieth century.

Catharine A. MacKinnon is Professor of Law at the University of Michigan and the University of Chicago. She is the author of *Sexual Harassment of Working Women,* which advocated making sexual harassment illegal as sex discrimination, as well as *Feminism Unmodified: Discourses on Life and Law* and *Toward a Feminist Theory of the State.* She and Andrea Dworkin wrote ordinances making pornography a violation of civil rights, and they are the co-authors of *Pornography and Civil Rights: A New Day for Women's Equality* and co-editors of *In Harm's Way: The Pornography Civil Rights Hearings.*

Michael A. Messner is Associate Professor of Sociology and Gender Studies at the University of Southern California. He has authored *Power at Play: Sports and the Problem of Masculinity* and co-authored *Sex, Violence, and Power in Sports: Rethinking Masculinity* (with Donald F. Sabo). His latest book is *Politics of Masculinities: Men in Movements* in the Sage Gender Lens series.

Sara Ruddick teaches at the Eugene Lang College of The New School for Social Research. She is the author of *Maternal Thinking: Toward a Politics of Peace.*

Paula C. Rust is Associate Professor at Hamilton College. She is a sociologist who specializes in the study of sexual identities and politics, with emphasis on bisexuality. She reached political consciousness during the height of lesbian feminism in the 1970s, and lives with her partner, Lorna, and their two children in an interracial, bicultural family.

Eve Kosofsky Sedgwick is the Newman Ivey White Professor of English at Duke University. She is the author of *The Coherence of Gothic Conventions, Between Men: English Literature and Male Homosocial Desire, Epistemology of the Closet,* and *Tendencies.*

Candace West is Professor of Sociology at the University of California, Santa Cruz. She is the author of *Routine Complications: Troubles with Talk Between Doctors and Patients,* as well as articles on language, gender, and conversational analysis and on the interactional basis for social structure.

Don H. Zimmerman is Professor of Sociology at the University of California, Santa Barbara. Other articles on gender co-authored with Candace West include "Sex Roles, Interruptions, and Silences," "Women's Place in Everyday Talk," and "Gender, Language, and Discourse."

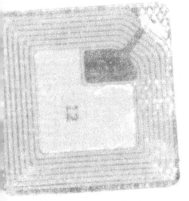

Part I

The Variety of Feminisms and Their Contributions to Gender Equality

Feminism is a social movement whose goal is raising the status of women. In many times and places in the past, men and women have proclaimed women's capabilities and have tried to better women's social position. As an organized movement, however, feminism rose in the nineteenth century in Europe and America.

A Brief History of Organized Feminism

The *first-wave* feminists of the nineteenth and early twentieth centuries fought for rights we take for granted today. It is hard to believe these rights were among those once denied to women of every social class, race, ethnicity, and religion—the right to vote (suffrage), to own property and capital, to inherit, to keep money earned, to go to college, to become a professionally certified physician, to argue cases in court.

The theory of equality that feminists of the nineteenth century used in their fight for women's rights came out of liberal political philosophy, which said that all men should be equal under the law, that no one should have special privileges or rights. Of course, when the United States of America was founded, that concept of equality excluded enslaved men and indentured men servants because they were not free citizens, as well as all women, no matter what their social status, because they were not really free either. Their legal status was the same as that of children—economically dependent and borrowing their social status from their father or husband. In Ibsen's famous play, *A Doll House*, Nora had to forge her dead father's signature because she could not legally sign her own name to the loan she needed to save her sick husband's life.

First-wave feminism's goal was to get equal rights for women, especially the vote, or suffrage. (Feminists were often called *suffragists*.) In the United States, women did not get the right to vote until 1919. Many European countries also gave women the right to vote after World War I, in repayment for their war efforts. French women, however, did not get suffrage until after World War II, when a grateful Charles de Gaulle enfranchised them for their work in the underground fight against the Nazis and the collaborationist government of occupied France.

The Russian and Chinese revolutions of the early twentieth century gave women equal rights, even though they criticized the individualism of "bourgeois feminism." Their emphasis was on work in the collective economy, with prenatal care and child care provided by the state so women could be both workers and mothers.

As the countries of Africa, Asia, and Central and South America broke free of colonial control after World War II and set up independent governments, they, too, gave their women citizens the right to vote. In some Muslim countries, however, women still cannot vote, leave the house without their husband's permission, drive cars, or appear in public unveiled.

Suffrage was the main goal of women's liberation in the first wave of feminism, but rights concerning property, earnings, and higher education—many of which were granted by the end of the nineteenth century—gave women a chance for economic independence. These rights were vital for raising married women's status from childlike dependence on a husband and for giving widows and single women some way of living on their own instead of as a poor relation in their father's or brother's or son's household. Liberated women in the first part of the twentieth century included independent factory girls who worked all day and went dancing at night, and middle- and upper-class educated women who had "Boston marriages," or open life-long companionships.

There was another branch of nineteenth-century feminism that did not focus on equal rights but on a woman's right to "own" her body and to plan her pregnancies. A feminist battle that was as hard fought as that for suffrage was the twentieth-century fight for legal means of contraception that could be controlled by the woman. Women could not be free to be good mothers and wives, especially if they were poor, if they had one child after another. But doctors were forbidden to fit women with diaphragms or cervical caps (the precursors of the coil and the pill). Even mailing information across state lines was illegal. The widespread use of contraception by married women was feared by traditionalists who saw the downfall of the family. Feminists feared that men would sexually exploit unmarried women who were protected against pregnancy. For women themselves, the positive outcome of this long battle for legalized woman-controlled contraception has been both greater sexual freedom before marriage and planned parenthood after marriage.

As is evident from this brief overview, the first-wave feminist movement had many of the theoretical and political differences of the feminist movement that succeeded it. The question of differences between women and men, and whether they should be treated *equally* because they are essentially the same or *equitably* because they are essentially different is still under debate. The question of where feminist politics should put the most effort—the public sphere (work and government) or the private sphere (family and sexuality)—is also still with us.

The current feminist movement is called the *second wave*. A post-World War II movement, it began with the publication in France in 1949 of Simone de Beauvoir's *The Second Sex*. This sweeping account of the historical and current status of women in the Western World argues that men set the standards and values and that women are the Other, those who lack the qualities the dominants exhibit. Men are the actors, women the reactors. Men thus are the first sex, women always the second sex. Men's dominance and women's subordination is not a biological phenomenon, de Beauvoir insisted, but a social creation: "One is not born, but rather becomes, a woman . . .; it is civilization as a whole that produces this creature . . . which is described as feminine" (1953, 267).

Although *The Second Sex* was widely read, the second wave of feminism did not take shape as an organized political movement until the 1960s, when young people were publicly criticizing many aspects of Western society. In the years since, feminism has made many contributions to social change by focusing attention on the continued ways women are more socially disadvantaged than men, by analyzing the sexual oppressions women suffer, and by proposing interpersonal as well as political and legal solutions. However, the feminist view of what makes women and men unequal is less unified today than in first-wave feminism, and there is a myriad of feminist solutions to gender inequality. If feminist voices seem to be much more fragmented than they were in the nineteenth century, it is the result of a deeper understanding of the sources of gender inequality. It is also the contradictory effect of uneven success. Feminists who are now parts of corporations, academia, or government, who are lawyers or doctors or respected artists and writers, are well aware of the limitations of their positions, given glass ceilings and sexual harassment. But their viewpoint is different from the more radical anti-establishment feminist critics who decry institutionalized sexual oppression and pervasive devaluation of women.

Although much of the feminist movement of the twentieth century has happened in industrialized countries, there have also been vital and important struggles for resources for girls and women in African and South American countries, especially after these countries became independent of their colonial masters. In the Middle East, women and men have struggled to reconcile the rights of women with the traditional precepts of Islam and Judaism. In Asia, the problems of poverty and overpopulation, even though they more often adversely affect women and girls, need remedies that affect everyone. Women's political movements in these countries may not be called "feminist," but they are gender-based battles nevertheless.

Further from the mainstream are feminisms that challenge "what everyone knows" about sex, sexuality, and gender—the duality and oppositeness of female and male, homosexual and heterosexual, women and men. These feminist theories are now being called the feminist *third wave;* they argue that there are many sexes, sexualities, and genders. If these ideas seem farfetched or outlandish, remember that at the beginning of the second wave, when feminists used "he or she" for the generic "he," "Ms" instead of "Miss" or "Mrs.," and "worker in the home" for "housewife," they were called radical troublemakers. Social change does not come without confrontation, and it is important to know what feminists who are not heard in the mass media are saying about gender inequality and how it can be eradicated.

Gender Inequality

The goal of feminism as a political movement is to make women and men more equal. *Gender inequality* takes many different forms, depending on the economic structure and social organization of a particular society and on the culture of any particular group within that society. Although we speak of *gender* inequality, it is usually women who are disadvantaged relative to similarly situated men. Women often receive lower pay for the same or comparable work, and they are frequently blocked in their chances for advancement, especially to top positions. There is usually an imbalance in the amount of housework and child care a wife does compared to her husband, even when both spend the same amount of time in paid work outside the home. When women professionals are matched with men of comparable productiveness, men still get greater recognition for their work and move up career ladders faster. On an overall basis, gender inequality means that work most often done by women, such as teaching small children and nursing, is paid less than work most often done by men, such as construction and mining. Gender inequality can also take the form of girls getting less education than boys of the same social class. It can mean that men get priority over women in the distribution of health care services and in the emphasis on research of men's diseases over women's.

Gender inequality takes even more oppressive and exploitative forms. Women are vulnerable to beatings, rape, and murder—often by their husbands or boyfriends, and especially when they try to leave an abusive relationship. The bodies of girls and women are used in sex work—pornography and prostitution. They are on display in movies, television, and advertising in Western cultures. In some African and Middle Eastern cultures their genitals are mutilated and their bodies are covered from head to toe in the name of chastity. They may be forced to bear children they do not want or to have abortions or be sterilized against their will. In countries with overpopulation, such as China, infant girls are much more often abandoned in orphanages than infant boys. In India, if the sex of the fetus can be determined, it is girls who are aborted.

Gender inequality can also disadvantage men. In many countries, only men serve in the armed forces, and in most countries, only men are sent into direct combat. It is mostly men who do the more dangerous work, such as firefighting and policing. Although women have fought in wars and are entering police forces and fire departments, the gender arrangements of most societies assume that women will do the work of bearing and caring for children while men will do the work of protecting and supporting them economically.

This gendered division of labor is rooted in the survival of small groups living at subsistence level, where babies are breastfed and food is obtained for older children and adults by foraging and hunting. The child-carers (mostly women) gathered fruits, vegetables, and hunted small animals—babies were carried in slings and older children were helpers. Those not caring for children (mostly men, but also unmarried women) could travel further in tracking large animals, more dangerous work. Hunters who came back with meat and hides were highly praised, but if the hunt was unsuccessful, they still had something to eat when they returned to the home camp, thanks to the child-minders' more reliable foraging.

Most women in industrial and post-industrial societies do not spend their lives having and caring for babies, and most women throughout the world do paid and unpaid work to supply their families with food, clothing, and shelter, even while they are taking care of children. The modern forms of gender inequality are not a complementary exchange of responsibilities but an elaborate system within which, it was estimated by a United Nations report in 1980, women do two-thirds of the world's work, receive 10 percent of the world's income, and own 1 percent of the world's property.

The major social and cultural institutions support this system of gender inequality. Religions legitimate the social arrangements that produce it, justifying them as right and proper. Laws support the status quo and also often make it impossible to redress the outcomes—to prosecute husbands for beating their wives, or boyfriends for raping their girlfriends. In the arts, women's productions are so often ignored that they are virtually invisible, leading author Virginia Woolf to conclude that Anonymous must have been a woman. Sciences have been accused of asking biased questions and ignoring findings that do not support conventional beliefs about sex differences.

Except for the Scandinavian countries, which have the greatest participation of women in government and the most gender-equal laws and state policies, most governments are run by socially dominant men, and their policies reflect their interests. In every period of change, including those of revolutionary upheaval, men's interests, not women's, have prevailed, and many men, but few women, have bene-fitted from progressive social policies. Equality and justice for all usually means for men only. Women have never had their revolution because the structure of gender as a social institution has never been seriously challenged. Therefore, all men benefit from the "patriarchal dividend"— women's unpaid work maintaining homes and bringing up children; women's low-paid work servicing hospitals, schools, and myriad other workplaces.

The main point recent feminisms have stressed about gender in-equality is that it is not an individual matter but is deeply ingrained in the structure of societies. Gender inequality is built into the organiza-tion of marriage and families, work and the economy, politics, religions, the arts and other cultural productions, and the very language we speak. Making women and men equal, therefore, necessitates social and not individual solutions.

Feminist Theories

The foregoing portrait of a gender-unequal world is a summation of the work of generations of feminist researchers and scholars. Femi-nist theories developed to explain the reasons for this pervasive gender inequality. Feminists are not satisfied with the explanation that it is natural, God-given, or necessary because women get pregnant and give birth and men do not. With deeper probing into the pervasiveness of gender inequality, feminists have produced more complex views about gender, sex, and sexuality. Although there is considerable overlap among them, it is useful to separate the concepts of gender, sex, and sexuality in order to illustrate how gendering modifies bodies and sexual behavior. This book uses the following definitions and vocabu-lary:

Gender: a social status and a personal identity, as enacted in parental and work roles and in relationships between women and men. Through the social processes of gendering, gender divisions and roles are built into the major social institutions of society, such as the econ-omy, the family, the state, culture, religion, and the law—the gendered social order. *Woman* and *man* are used when referring to gender.

Sex: a complex interplay of genes, hormones, environment, and behavior, with loop-back effects between bodies and society. *Male* and *female* are used when referring to sex.

Sexuality: lustful desire, emotional involvement, and fantasy, as enacted in a variety of long- and short-term intimate relationships. *Homosexuality* and *heterosexuality* are used when referring to sexuality.

Third-wave feminism has concentrated on examining the complex interplay of sex, sexuality, and gender. These feminists speak of genders, sexes, and sexualities. The two "opposites" in each case—women and men, female and male, homosexual and heterosexual—have become multiple. These feminists point to recent research that has shown female and male physiology to be produced and maintained by both female and male hormones. They argue that sex is more of a continuum than a sharp dichotomy. Similarly, studies of sexual orientation have shown that neither homosexuality nor heterosexuality is always fixed for life, and that bisexuality, in feelings and in sexual relationships, is widespread. When it comes to gender, many third-wave feminist social researchers prefer to speak of genders, since men's and women's social statuses, personal identities, and life chances are intricately tied up with their racial, ethnic, and religious groups, their social class, their family background, and their place of residence.

Nonetheless, these widely differing groups of people have to fit into two and only two genders in Western societies—"men" and "women." These two major status categories are supposed to be different from each other, and the members of each category are supposed to have essential similarities. Work and family roles, as well as practically all other aspects of social life, are built on these two major divisions of people. This gendering produces the *gendered social order.*

Given the variety of feminist theories about the main sources of gender inequality, it would be better to speak of *feminisms,* rather than feminism. The feminisms of the last half-century can be grouped into three broad categories that reflect their approaches to gender inequality. These are *gender reform feminisms, gender resistance feminisms,* and *gender rebellion feminisms.* Gender reform feminisms want to change the content but not the structure of the gendered social order; for example, they want to see more women as presidents of major corporations. Gender resistance feminisms think that the gendered social order is so oppressive to women that women should not cooperate with it. Gender rebellion feminisms challenge the structure of the gendered social order by questioning its basis—the division of people into two genders.

Types of Feminisms

In this book, current feminisms are categorized according to their *theory or theories of gender inequality*—what they consider the main reason for women having a lesser social status and fewer advantages than men of similar education, class background, religion, race, and ethnic group. From these theories follow the feminism's proposed solutions or remedies—its *politics*. Feminist politics does not refer only to the arena of government or the law; it can be confrontational protests, such as Take Back the Night marches, or work through organizations with a broad base, such as the National Organization of Women (NOW) and the National Organization for Men Against Sexism (NOMAS). It can be service centers, such as battered women's shelters, and service activities, such as gender-sensitivity and anti-rape sessions for college men. Changing language and media presentations to remove sexist putdowns that denigrate men as well as women is also feminist politics. Other remedies for redressing gender inequality, such as creating culture and knowledge from a woman's point of view, may not look political, but to feminists, they are deeply political because their intent is to change the way people look at the world.

In an overall sense, the politics of each group of feminisms takes its emphasis from the feminism's theoretical focus. Gender reform feminisms focus on women's work in the family and the economy. Gender resistance feminisms focus on violence and sexual oppression against women, and on making women's experiences central to knowledge and culture. Gender rebellion feminisms focus on the processes and symbols that build and maintain the gender order.

Gender reform feminisms (liberal, marxist and socialist, development) have made visible the pervasiveness of overt discriminatory practices, both formal and informal. The 1960s and 1970s brought dissatisfaction with conventional ideas about women and men, their bodies, sexualities, psyches, and behavior. The beliefs prevalent at that time about women and men tended to stress differences between them, and to denigrate women in comparison with men, who were seen as stronger, smarter, and generally more capable than women—except for taking care of children. Mothering was women's strength and responsibility, and so women were seen as mothers before, during, and after they were anything else.

Gender reform feminisms want women to be valued as much as men and to be free to live their lives according to their *human* potential.

People should be able to work, parent, produce culture and science, govern, and otherwise engage in social life as they choose, whether they are women or men. The goal of gender reform feminisms is equal participation of women and men in all walks of life.

Gender resistance feminisms (radical, lesbian, psychoanalytic, standpoint) claim that the gender order cannot be made gender-neutral because men's dominance is too strong. Gender equality, they argue, ends up with women becoming just like men—career-oriented and unemotional. They stress the importance of a perspective based on women's experience. By examining the gender order from the standpoint of women, they make visible the hidden relationships among organizations, institutions, and daily practices that allow men to control women's lives. They call it *patriarchy,* a concept referring to men's pervasive domination introduced by marxist feminism.

In the 1970s and 1980s, gender resistance feminisms developed an important theoretical insight—the power of *gender ideology*, the values and beliefs that justify the gendered social order. Gender resistance feminisms argue that gender inequality has been legitimated by major religions that say men's dominance is a reflection of God's will; by sciences that claim the dominance is a result of genetic or hormonal differences; and by legal systems that deny women redress in the courts. The mass media, sports, and pornography encourage the excesses of men's power—violence, rape, and sexual exploitation.

Some feminists feel that men's oppression of women is so universal that the best way to resist is to form a woman-centered society and create a women-oriented culture, ethics, and even religion. This strategy is called *cultural feminism.* It is not really a separate feminism but a trend within radical and lesbian feminism. Other gender resistance feminists say that the systemic violence against women and exploitation of women's sexuality needs continued political engagement with the larger society, at the same time as woman-only spaces are created for refuge and recreation. All the gender resistance feminisms stress the importance of countering the negative evaluations of women by valorizing their nurturance, emotional supportiveness, and mothering capacities; encouraging pride in women's bodies; and by teaching women how to protect themselves against sexual violence.

Gender rebellion feminisms (multiracial, men, social construction, postmodern, and queer theory) attack the gender order directly by undermining the boundaries between women and men, female and male, heterosexual and homosexual. Since the 1980s, feminist deconstruction of the categories of sex, sexuality, and gender has shown how their taken-for-grantedness maintains the gender order. By questioning the dualities of male and female, heterosexual and homosexual, masculine and feminine, man and woman, gender rebellion feminisms undermine the legitimacy of favoring one group over its opposite.

Gender rebellion feminisms trace the connections among gender, race, ethnicity, religion, social class, and sexual orientation to show how people become advantaged or disadvantaged in complex stratification systems. The gendered social order, they argue, sets men against men as well as men against women. Men and women of the same racial and ethnic group or in the same economic stratum have much in common with each other, more than men may have with men or women with women in other groups. Sexual orientation also divides groups of women and men, with gay men and lesbian women splitting off and forming their own communities. But gays and lesbians together also form homosexual-rights coalitions and work together in AIDS service organizations.

Thus, according to gender rebellion feminism, both personal identities and the identity politics of groups are constantly shifting. There is room in life for individual and social change, for new kinds of relationships, and for new ways of organizing work and family.

All the feminisms have made important contributions to improving women's status, but each also has limitations. Indeed, feminist theories have changed as the limitations of one set of ideas were critiqued and addressed by what was felt to be a better explanation about why women and men were so unequal in status and power. But it has not been a clear progression by any means, because many of the debates went on simultaneously. As a matter of fact, many are still going on. And because all of the feminisms have insight into the problems of gender inequality, and all have come up with good strategies for remedying these problems, all the feminisms are still very much with us. There are continuities and convergences, as well as sharp debates, among the different feminisms.

Organization of the Book

The focus of this book is the continuities, discontinuities, and convergences in recent feminist theories and politics. I will be combining ideas from different feminist writers, and usually will not be talking about any specific writers, except for the excerpted authors. A list of readings can be found at the end of each chapter.

Because I am not examining the ideas of particular feminists but speaking of ideas that have emerged from many theorists, I will talk of feminisms rather than feminists. Any feminist may incorporate ideas and politics from several feminisms, and many feminists have shifted their views over the years. I myself was originally a liberal feminist, then a socialist feminist, and now consider myself to be primarily a gender rebellion feminist.

What I am looking at first is *feminist theories* about why women and men are unequal, and second, *feminist politics*, the activities and strategies for remedying gender inequality. Feminist theories and politics are the result of personal experiences shared among friends and in consciousness-raising groups. They are developed in classes and conferences on all kinds of topics. They are refined in journals and books. And they are translated into political action through large and small feminist organizations, in marches and voting booths, in the marble halls of the United Nations and in grass-roots efforts in urban racial ethnic ghettos and developing countries of Africa, South and Central America, and Asia.

In Parts Two through Four, the theories and politics of *gender reform, gender resistance,* and *gender rebellion feminisms* are first described in a general way, followed by more detailed descriptions of the feminisms within the larger grouping. Each discussion of a particular feminism begins with an outline of its attribution of the main causes of gender inequality, its recommendation for remedies, and its contributions to social change. The discussion of each type of feminism includes two excerpts from feminist theorists who use that viewpoint. Each chapter ends with a discussion of the feminism's theoretical and political limitations.

In the final section, Feminism's Future, I present my own ideas about fruitful theoretical and political directions for feminism. These ideas are based for the most part in the gender rebellion feminisms discussed in Part Four.

Suggested Readings—Overviews and History

Bernard, Jessie. 1981. *The Female World.* New York: Free Press.

Chafetz, Janet Saltzman, and Anthony Gary Dworkin. 1986. *Female Revolt: Women's Movements in World and Historical Perspective.* Totowa, NJ: Rowman & Allanheld.

de Beauvoir, Simone. [1949] 1953. *The Second Sex.* (Trans. by H. M. Parshley). New York: Knopf.

Evans, Judith. 1995. *Feminist Theory Today: An Introduction to Second-Wave Feminism.* Newbury Park, CA: Sage.

Gordon, Linda. 1990. *Woman's Body, Woman's Right: Birth Control in America.* (Rev. ed.). Baltimore, MD: Penguin.

Jaggar, Alison M. 1983. *Feminist Politics and Human Nature.* Totowa, NJ: Rowman & Allanheld.

Kraditor, Aileen S. 1981. *The Ideas of the Woman Suffrage Movement/1890–1920.* New York: W. W. Norton.

Mohanty, Chandra Talpade, Ann Russo, and Lourdes Torres (eds.). 1991. *Third World Women and the Politics of Feminism.* Bloomington: Indiana University Press.

Moi, Toril. 1985. *Sexual/Textual Politics: Feminist Literary Theory.* New York: Methuen.

Rossi, Alice S. (ed.). 1973. *The Feminist Papers: From Adams to de Beauvoir.* New York: Columbia University Press.

Showalter, Elaine (ed.). 1985. *The New Feminist Criticism: Essays on Women, Literature, and Theory.* New York: Pantheon.

Tong, Rosemarie. 1989. *Feminist Thought: A Comprehensive Introduction.* Boulder, CO: Westview Press.

Warhol, Robyn R., and Diane Price Herndl. 1991. *Feminisms: An Anthology of Literary Theory and Criticism.* New Brunswick, NJ: Rutgers University Press.

Woolf, Virginia. 1929 [1957]. *A Room of One's Own.* New York: Harcourt, Brace & World.

Part II

Gender Reform Feminisms

Overview

The feminisms of the 1960s and 1970s were the beginning of the *second wave* of feminism. (Part One gives a brief history of the first wave.) Liberal feminism's roots were in eighteenth and nineteenth century liberal political philosophies that developed the idea of individual rights; marxist and socialist feminisms' base was Marx's nineteenth century critique of capitalism and his concept of class consciousness; development feminism used twentieth century anti-colonial politics and ideas of national development. These earlier works were mostly about men. Gender reform feminisms put women into these perspectives.

Liberal feminism claims that gender differences are not based in biology and therefore that women and men are not all that different: their common humanity supersedes their procreative differences. If women and men are not so different, then they should not be treated differently under the law. Women should have the same legal rights as men and the same educational and work opportunities.

Marxist and socialist feminisms argue that the source of women's oppression is their economic dependence on a husband and their exploitation as cheap labor in the capitalist workforce because they are seen primarily as wives and mothers. The solution is full-time jobs for women, with the state providing paid maternity leave and childcare. This feminism recognizes that what the state gives, the state can take away. State policies reflect state interests, not women's. Women are worker-mothers or just mothers, depending on the state's economic and procreative needs.

Women's work for the family and men's production work give each of them different consciousnesses. Women are grounded in everyday life and in emotional relationships; men are detached and inexpressive. These diametrically opposed ways of thinking and feeling, plus women's and men's different interests as wife-mother or breadwinner make the family a terrain for conflict and power struggles.

For *development feminism*, the theoretical emphasis on universal human rights is reflected in developing countries in political pressure for the education of girls, maternity and child health care, and economic resources for women who contribute heavily to the support of their families. However, when feminist gender politics calls for wives and husbands to be equal, and for women to have sexual autonomy, development feminism frequently has to confront traditional cultural values and practices that give men power over their daughters and wives. The women's own solution to this dilemma is community organizing around their family roles.

All of the gender reform feminisms have revolutionary potential because they address the basic structure of the gendered social order— the division of labor between women and men. They all see men as advantaged in the sphere of paid work, in that they usually have better jobs and are paid more than women. Theoretically, men's work should allow them to support a wife and children, but throughout the world and throughout history, women have taken care of children and also produced food, clothing, and other material necessities, as part of their work for their family.

When the industrial revolution moved the production of commodities outside of the home into the factory, not only men, but women and children, went out to work for wages. The men who could support their families completely were the factory owners and those who had inherited wealth, and their wives were expected to be hostesses and supervisors of the household servants. By the middle of the twentieth century, working-class women were still juggling family work and paid work to supplement the family income, and middle-class, college educated women were languishing in the suburbs, feeling useless once their children were in school.

It is this historically intertwined structure of work and family and women's roles within it that gender reform feminisms tackle. But their political solutions leave the gendered structure of family work intact and concentrate on raising women's low economic status through paid work and state-provided children's benefits. Such reforms have to be tailored to a society's economic development. Even within the same country, what works for the women of one class or racial ethnic group is not necessarily going to work for another. Women of disadvantaged racial and ethnic groups who have to work at low-level factory or service jobs to keep food on the table may see being "just a housewife" as utopia. Similarly, women in the former communist countries envied the stable marriages of women in capitalist countries, who, in turn, envied the state supports for child care and encouragement to hold full-time jobs. However, as women in countries at all different stages of industrial development have seen, the success of their fight for gender equality in the paid workplace depends enormously on a high level of economic prosperity.

Chapter One

Liberal Feminism

Sources of Gender Inequality

- Gender stereotyping and devaluation of women
- Division of work into women's jobs and men's jobs
- Low pay for women's jobs
- Restricted entry into top positions (*glass ceiling*)
- Lack of affordable child care for mothers who work outside the home
- Limitations on reproductive choice

Remedies

- Gender-neutral childrearing and education
- Bringing women into occupations and professions dominated by men and breaking through the glass ceiling to positions of authority (*affirmative action*)
- More women in politics
- Shared parenting and employer-financed child care
- Legal, accessible, and affordable reproductive services

Contributions

- Calling attention to gender discrimination and gender stereotyping in workplaces and in education

- Making language more gender-neutral
- Working with civil rights organizations to frame affirmative action guidelines and to bring lawsuits for women and disadvantaged men
- Encouraging employers to provide workplace childcare and paid parental leave
- Getting more women elected and appointed to governmental positions
- Getting abortion legalized in the United States

In the 1960s and 1970s, the feminist focus in the United States was on women as individuals and the narrowness of their lives. Liberal feminism's complaint that women were confined to a main "job" of wife-mother, with anything else they did having to take a back seat to child care and housework, was the theme of Betty Friedan's best-selling book, *The Feminine Mystique*. Women who wanted careers or who were ambitious to make a mark in the arts or in politics were suspect unless they were also "good" wives and mothers (especially mothers). Another problem that kept women down was men's devaluation of them as not too bright, clothes-conscious, and overly emotional. Of course, these impressions were exactly what a woman was taught to convey to a man if she wanted to get a husband.

In many ways, the early appeals of liberal feminism to men were open and straightforward—stop calling a wife "the little woman," recognize our past achievements and capabilities in many fields, let us do the kind of work we want outside the home, share some of the housework and childcare, legalize abortion. It does not sound very earth-shaking today, because so many of these goals have been achieved. Women have entered every field, from mining to space travel. Women in the police force and the military are no longer an oddity, and women in high positions, including leaders of countries, are no longer a rarity.

Other liberal feminist goals are still being debated. One is the question of whether men can be as good at parenting as women. Liberal feminism argues that gendered characteristics, such as women's parenting abilities, may seem biological but are really social products. Their proof that mothering skills are learned and not inborn, for example, is that men learn them, too, when they end up with responsibility for raising children alone. But when there is a woman around, the assumption is that she is better at childcare than any man, and so women end up doing most of the physically and emotionally intensive work of bringing up children.

A second continuing problem is that families, teachers, picture books, school books, and the mass media still encourage boys to be "masculine" and girls to be "feminine," even when they show adult women and men acting in more gender-neutral ways. Gender inequality is built into this socialization because supposedly masculine characteristics, such as assertiveness, are more highly valued than supposedly feminine characteristics, such as emotional supportiveness. Liberal feminism promotes nonsexist socialization and education of children as well as media presentations of men and women in nontraditional roles, especially men as caring and competent fathers. These areas still need constant monitoring—computer software programs for girls feature sexy Barbie dolls and kissing skills, while boys' computer games feature violent adventure fantasies.

The workplace is another area where liberal feminism has made important contributions, but where women are still a long way from gender equality. Thanks to feminist pressure, more and more women have entered fields formerly dominated by men, such as the sciences, and women in positions of authority are not the big news they once were. However, sexist patterns of hiring and promotion still produce workplaces where men and women work at different jobs and where most of the top positions are held by men. Liberal feminism has developed important theories to explain the persistence of the *gender segregation* of jobs (men work with men and women work with women), and the *gender stratification* of organizational hierarchies (the top of the pyramid is invariably almost all men).

The theory of *gendered job queues* argues that the best jobs are kept for men of the dominant racial ethnic group. When a job no longer pays well or has deteriorating working conditions, dominant men leave for other work, and men of disadvantaged racial ethnic groups and all women can move into them. Occupations stay segregated, but who does the job changes. Some jobs have shifted from men's work to women's work within a decade. A typical case is bank teller in the United States.

Disadvantaged groups of workers continue to get lower pay and have poorer working conditions than the dominant group because the new crop of "best jobs" again goes to the most advantaged group of workers. Thus, in the United States, White men monopolize the most lucrative financial and computer jobs.

The strategy of *affirmative action* was developed to redress the gender, race, and ethnic imbalance in workplaces, schools, and job-training programs. Affirmative action programs develop a diversified pool of qualified people by encouraging men to train for such jobs as nurse, elementary school teacher, and secretary, and women to go into fields like engineering, construction, and police work. Employers are legally mandated to hire enough workers of different races and genders to achieve a reasonable balance in their workforce. The law also requires employers to pay the workers the same and to give them an equal chance to advance in their careers.

With regard to gender, this change in numbers of women in a workplace was supposed to have a psychological effect on both men and women. Earlier theories had argued that women were not aggressive about competing with men on the job or at school because they feared that success would make them so disliked that they would never have a social life. Rosabeth Moss Kanter, a sociologist and management researcher, said that it was token status as the lone woman among men, visible and vulnerable, that created women's fears. The *Kanter hypothesis* predicted that as workplaces became more gender-balanced, men would become more accepting of women colleagues, and women would have other women to bond with instead of having to go it alone as the single token woman. The following excerpt from her influential book, *Men and Women of the Corporation,* lays out Moss Kanter's hypothesis about the effect of numbers of women on the culture and social structure of a workplace.

NUMBERS: MINORITIES AND MAJORITIES

Rosabeth Moss Kanter

... Yet questions of how many and how few confound any statements about the organizational behavior of special kinds of people. For example, certain popular conclusions and research findings about male-female relations or role potentials may turn critically on the issue of proportions. One study of mock jury deliberations found that men played proactive, task-oriented leadership roles, whereas women in the

same groups tended to take reactive, emotional, and nurturant pos-
tures—supposed proof that traditional stereotypes reflect behavior realities. But, strikingly, *men far outnumbered women in all of the groups
studied.* Perhaps it was the women's scarcity that pushed them into
classical positions and the men's numerical superiority that encouraged
them to assert task superiority. Similarly, the early kibbutzim, collective
villages in Israel that theoretically espoused equality of the sexes but
were unable to fully implement it, could push women into traditional
service positions because there were *more than twice as many men as
women.* Again, relative numbers interfered with a fair test of what men
or women can "naturally" do, as it did in the case of the relatively few
women in the upper levels of Indsco. Indeed, recently Marcia Guttentag
has found sex ratios in the population in general to be so important
that they predict a large number of behavioral phenomena, from the
degree of power women and men feel to the ways they cope with the
economic and sexual aspects of their lives.

To understand the dramas of the many and the few in the organization requires a theory and a vocabulary. Four group types can be
identified on the basis of different proportional representations of kinds
of people. . . . *Uniform* groups have only one kind of person, one significant social type. The group may develop its own differentiations, of
course, but groups called uniform can be considered homogeneous
with respect to salient external master statuses such as sex, race, or
ethnicity. Uniform groups have a typological ratio of 100:0. *Skewed*
groups are those in which there is a large preponderance of one type
over another, tip to a ratio of perhaps 85:15. The numerically dominant
types also control the group and its culture in enough ways to be labeled
"dominants." The few of another type in a skewed group can appropriately be called "tokens," for . . . they are often treated as representatives
of their category, as symbols rather than individuals. If the absolute size
of the skewed group is small, tokens can also be solos, the only one of
their kind present; but even if there are two tokens in a skewed group,
it is difficult for them to generate an alliance that can become powerful
in the group. . . . Next, *tilted* groups begin to move toward less extreme
distributions and less exaggerated effects. In this situation, with ratios
of perhaps 65:35, dominants are just a "majority" and tokens become
a "minority." Minority members have potential allies among each other,
can form coalitions, and can affect the culture of the group. They begin
to become individuals differentiated from each other as well as a type
differentiated from the majority. Finally, at about 60:40 and down to

50:50, the group becomes *balanced.* Culture and interaction reflect this balance. Majority and minority turn into potential subgroups that may or may not generate actual type-based identifications. Outcomes for individuals in such a balanced peer group, regardless of type, will depend more on other structural and personal factors, including formation of subgroups or differentiated roles and abilities.

It is the characteristics of the second type, the skewed group, that underlay the behavior and treatment of professional and managerial women observed at Indsco. If the ratio of women to men in various parts of the organization begins to shift, as affirmative action and new hiring and promotion policies promised, forms of relationships and peer culture should also change. But as of the mid-1970s, the dynamics of tokenism predominated in Indsco's . . . ranks, and women and men were in the positions of token and dominant. Tokenism, like low opportunity and low power, set in motion self-perpetuating cycles that served to reinforce the low numbers of women and, in the absence of external intervention, to keep women in the position of token.

The recognition that a token or two did not make for a truly diversified workplace provided the impetus for affirmative action. The goal is not perfect balance but a workplace where different kinds of people are fully integrated and respected colleagues. The Kanter hypothesis predicts a positive attitude change when a formerly imbalanced workplace becomes more gender-balanced. However, later research found that as more women enter, there is often a backlash in the form of increasing sexual harassment and denigration of women's capabilities—a defense against what is felt to be the encroachment of women on men's territory. Men's stonewalling is particularly likely when women are competing with them for jobs on the fast track up the career ladder.

The concept of *gatekeeping* explains how most women are kept from getting to the top in occupations and professions dominated by men. Gatekeeping used to keep women out of male-dominated fields entirely. Now gatekeeping keeps women out of the line for promotion to the top positions. The ways that most people move up in their careers are through *networking* (finding out about job and promotion opportunities through word-of-mouth and being recommended by someone already there) and *mentoring* (being coached by a protective senior to understand the informal norms of the workplace). Becoming part of a network and getting a mentor are made much easier if you become a *protégé* of a senior colleague.

In many fields, hiring and promotion decisions are not made strictly on the basis of merit but through the help and support of "godfathers" or "rabbis" who take younger people under their wing as protégés and invite them into the "inner circles" where information is traded and deals are cut. Because senior members of an organization are looking for people to eventually succeed them, they usually choose as protégés those who are similar to themselves in race, ethnicity, religion, and gender. The exclusivity of the protégé system and its discriminatory role in sorting out people who "don't belong" has for years come under attack by liberal feminism.

Cynthia Fuchs Epstein, a sociologist who has done extensive research on women lawyers, has documented the difficulties even well-trained professional women have in making careers because they are excluded from the informal protégé system and from men's clubs.

THE PROTÉGÉ SYSTEM

Cynthia Fuchs Epstein

The protégé system is typical of many professions, especially in their upper reaches. It operates both to train personnel in certain specialties and to assure continuity of leadership. The fields in which it exists are marked by interplay between the formal and informal relationships of the practitioners. At certain levels one must be "in" to learn the job. . . .

The sponsor-protégé, or master-apprentice, relationship may inhibit feminine advancement in the professions. The sponsor is most likely to be a man and will tend to have mixed feelings, among them a nagging sense of impending trouble, about accepting a woman as a protégé. Although the professional man might not object to a female assistant—he might even prefer her—he cannot identify her (as he might a male assistant) as someone who will eventually be his successor. He will usually prefer a male candidate in the belief that the woman has less commitment and will easily be deflected from her career by marriage and children. This presumed lack of commitment is troublesome in the relationship even if the woman is accepted as an apprentice or a protégé.

She may be under considerable strain because the sponsor may be oblivious of her other role demands. In addition, her other role partners—husband, father, child—may be suspicious or resentful of her loyalty to and dependence on the sponsor. The sponsor's wife may also be suspicious of the ties between the sponsor and his female protégé. Many professional men feel it is wiser to avoid this kind of domestic trouble.

Even if she serves an apprenticeship, the woman faces serious problems at the next step in her career if she does not get the sponsor's support for entrée to the inner circles of the profession—support that a male apprentice would expect as a matter of course. The sponsor may exert less effort in promoting a woman for a career-line job. He may feel less responsibility for her career because he assumes she is not as dependent on a career as a man might be. . . .

Because of the woman's presumed lack of commitment and drive, the sponsor may be reluctant to present her to colleagues as a reliable candidate for their long-term enterprises. It is true, however, that if a woman can enter into a protégé relationship it may be more important for her than for a man, and that a male sponsor may make an extra effort to promote the female protégée because he is aware of the difficulties she is apt to face. In fact, she may be able to rise or gain notice in a field only because she is a protégée, although this form of entrée is not typical or necessary for men.

We cannot specify the conditions under which one or the other pattern will prevail. It is probably highly contingent on the social structure of the discipline or specialty in which the relationship arises, the personalities of the sponsor and protégée, and, of course, the quality of the woman's talent as well as her personality and physical attractiveness. . . .

In many professions, men have chosen to conduct their business in men's faculty and university clubs, men's bars, golf and athletic clubs, and during poker games. In addition, many once informal traditions have developed into rigidly formalized male cults, as, for example, the academic "high table" in the colleges of Cambridge and Oxford. Obstacles abound not only for females aspiring to membership in such groups, but also for males from an alien social class or social tradition. Informal systems of introduction and support abound in the job markets of many countries (Mexico and Israel are two), but not in the United States and other nations where technical skills count most. In the United States, ability and achievement alone may only occasionally suffice to insure a good career; the talented but retiring and the promising but nonconforming may simply fall by the wayside.

The only possible antidote for the familiarity and lineage which oil the wheels in professional environments is power through rank, seniority, money, or charisma; women do not often have any of these defenses. . . .

Eminence also often correlates with age, which may further reduce the focus placed on sex status. Many of the feminine role components attached to the female sex status become less intrusive in interactions between men and women as the woman grows older; it is probably accurate to suppose that in most cases as the woman ages, her sexual appeal becomes less an object of focus. Since a woman is apt to encounter resistance if her professional status requires the exercise of authority over others, she may find that she can depend on deriving a certain amount of authority from her age. While a man might resent "taking orders" from a woman, he probably would be less resistant if the woman is older. Thus, the woman needs not only the rank which derives from her status as an expert, but also that from her age status. Correlatively, when the woman is younger than the man, or the same age, she is more apt to encounter resistance to her authority. . . .

Reprinted from: Cynthia Fuchs Epstein, *Woman's Place: Options and Limits in Professional Careers,* pp. 168–70, 174. Copyright © 1971 by Regents of the University of California and the University of California Press. Reprinted by permission.

In professions and in managerial positions, where jobs pay the best, have the most prestige, and command the most authority, few senior men take on women as their protégées. As a result, there has been a *glass ceiling* on the advancement of women in every field they have entered in the last 25 years. The concept of the glass ceiling assumes that women have the motivation, ambition, and capacity for positions of power and prestige, but hidden barriers keep them from reaching the top. They can see their way to their goal, but they bump their heads on a ceiling that is both invisible and impenetrable. Similar processes of informal discrimination hinder the careers of men of disadvantaged groups as well; women of color have had to face both racism and sexism.

Critique. There is an internal theoretical contradiction in liberal feminism that centers on the question of whether women and men have to be the same to be equal. The campaign to bring up children in a gender-neutral way has meant encouraging a mixture of existing masculine and feminine characteristics and traits (*androgyny*) that boys and girls will be similar in personalities and behavior. The corollary campaign to integrate women into all parts of public life, especially the workplace, and for men to share parenting and other roles in private life, means that women and men can be interchangeable.

The logical outcome of liberal feminism is a genderless society, one not based on women and men as socially meaningful categories. But because of men's social domination, the actual thrust of both gender-neutrality and integration is often the continued predominance of masculine traits and values, such as devotion to a career, with the consequence that women become like men. For this reason, liberal feminism has been accused of denigrating *womanliness* (nurturance, empathy, an ethics of care) and pregnancy and childbirth in their fight to advance the social status of women.

The goal of liberal feminism in the United States was embodied in the Equal Rights Amendment to the U.S. Constitution, which was never ratified. It said, "Equality of rights under the law shall not be denied or abridged by the United States or any state on account of sex." The negative response of the American public to the Equal Rights Amendment may have been a gut reaction to the genderless possibilities of an absolutely even-handed legal status for women and men. When laws speak of "pregnant persons," as did a Supreme Court decision equating pregnancy with disability or illness, many people, including feminists, feel that androgyny has gone too far.

Summary

The main contribution of liberal feminism has been to show how much modern society discriminates against women by insisting that women and men must be treated differently. Liberal feminist theory says that biological differences should be ignored in order to achieve gender equality. Women and men should be treated in a gender-neutral manner, especially under the law.

In the United States, liberal feminism has been successful in breaking down many barriers to women's entry into formerly male-dominated jobs and professions, in helping to equalize wage scales, and in legalizing abortion. But liberal feminism has not been able to overcome the prevailing belief that women and men are intrinsically different. Although gender differences can co-exist with equitable or even-handed treatment, the way women are treated in modern society, especially in the workplace, still produces large gaps in salaries, job opportunities, and advancement.

Politically, liberal feminism's focus has been on visible sources of gender discrimination, such as gendered job markets and inequitable wage scales, and with getting women into positions of authority in the professions, government, and cultural institutions. Liberal feminist politics takes important weapons of the civil rights movement—anti-discrimination legislation and affirmative action programs—and uses them to fight gender inequality, especially in the job market. Liberal feminism has been less successful in fighting the informal processes of discrimination and exclusion that have produced the glass ceiling so many women face in their career advancement.

The great strides that women of the last generation have made have led many young people to think that feminism is passé. But the gender equality in the workplace and the home that liberal feminism achieved is concentrated in the United States in the middle and upper class, where people who are more likely to have good jobs, steady incomes, and live in two-parent households. The Scandinavian countries have achieved gender equality through welfare-state benefits to everyone, and also have many more women in government and in policy-making positions than the rest of the world, including North America and much of the rest of Europe.

Most of the world's women, however, live in countries where only a very small group of people have a high standard of living. Their economic and social problems produce a level of gender inequality that needs quite different feminist theories and politics.

Suggested Readings in Liberal Feminism

Bartlett, Katharine T., and Rosanne Kennedy (eds.). 1991. *Feminist Legal Theory: Readings in Law and Gender.* Boulder, CO: Westview Press.

Eisenstein, Zillah. 1981. *The Radical Future of Liberal Feminism.* New York: Longman.

Epstein, Cynthia Fuchs. 1971. *Women's Place: Options and Limits in Professional Careers.* Berkeley: University of California Press.

——. 1988. *Deceptive Distinctions: Sex, Gender and the Social Order.* New Haven, CT: Yale University Press.

Friedan, Betty. 1963. *The Feminine Mystique.* New York: W. W. Norton.

Kanter, Rosabeth Moss. 1977. *Men and Women of the Corporation.* New York: Basic Books.

Lamb, Michael E. 1987 (ed.). *The Father's Role: Cross-cultural Perspectives.* Hillsdale, NJ: Lawrence Erlbaum.

Reskin, Barbara F., and Patricia A. Roos. 1990. *Job Queues, Gender Queues: Explaining Women's Inroads into Male Occupations.* Philadelphia: Temple University Press.

Tuchman, Gaye, Arlene Kaplan Daniels, and James Benet. 1978. *Hearth and Home: Images of Women in the Mass Media.* New York: Oxford University Press.

Weisberg, D. Kelly (ed.). 1993. *Feminist Legal Theory: Foundations.* Philadelphia: Temple University Press.

Chapter Two

Marxist and Socialist Feminism

Sources of Gender Inequality

- Exploitation of women in unwaged work for the family
- Use of women workers as a *reserve army of labor*—hired when the economy needs workers, fired when it does not
- Low pay for women's jobs

Remedies

- Government-subsidized maternal and child healthcare, childcare services, financial allowances for children, free education
- Permanent waged work for women
- Comparable worth programs to equalize salaries of men's and women's jobs

Contributions

- Gender analysis putting women as paid and unpaid workers into capitalist and socialist economies

- Making visible the necessity and worth of women's unpaid work in the home to the functioning of industrial economies and to the social reproduction of future workers
- Getting government-subsidized maternal and child services in social-welfare states and in the former communist countries

During the 1970s, marxist and socialist feminist theories blamed the economic structure and the material aspects of life as the main source of gender inequality. These theories are grounded in historical materialism, which says that every major change in production—from hunting and gathering to farming to the industrial revolution—changes the social organization of work and family. In preindustrial societies, women's domestic labor not only maintained the home and brought up the children but also entailed getting or growing food, making cloth and sewing clothing, and other work that allowed the family to subsist. This work was done side by side with the men and children of the family. The industrial revolution of the nineteenth century brought a major change—the removal of production work from the home to factories, and the change from making household goods at home to their becoming mass-produced commodities. The means of production, then, were no longer owned by the worker but by capitalists, who hired workers at wages low enough to make a profit.

Marx's analysis of the social structure of capitalism was supposed to apply to people of any social characteristics. If you owned the means of production, you were a member of the capitalist class; if you sold your labor for a wage, you were a member of the proletariat. That should be true of women as well, except that until the end of the nineteenth century, married women in capitalist countries were not allowed to own property in their own name; any wages they earned and their profits from any businesses they ran belonged legally to their husband.

Although Marx and other nineteenth-century economic theorists recognized the exploitation of wives' domestic labor, it was marxist feminism that put housewives at the forefront of its analysis of the gendered structure of capitalism. Housewives are vital to capitalism, indeed to any industrial economy, because their unpaid work in the home maintains bosses and workers and reproduces the next generation of bosses and workers (and their wives). Furthermore, if a bourgeois husband falls on hard times, his wife can do genteel work in the home, such as dressmaking, to earn extra money, or can take a temporary or part-time white-collar job. And when a worker's wages fall below the level needed to feed his family, as it often does, his wife can go out to work for wages in a factory or shop or another person's home, or she can turn the home into a small factory and put everyone, sometimes including the children, to work. The housewife's labor, paid and unpaid, is for her family. Marxist feminism argues that this exploitation of women's work, both in the home and in the marketplace, is the prime source of gender inequality.

Marxist feminism analyzes the ways in which two parallel institutions—the economy (capitalism) and the family (patriarchy)—structure women's and men's lives. A man who works for wages is exploited by capitalism because he is never paid as much as the profits he produces. At home, however, he has someone to work for him—his wife. She cooks his food, washes his clothing, satisfies his sexual needs, and brings up his children. If he loses his job, or cannot earn enough to support his family, she will go out to work or take work into the home, but she will continue her domestic duties as well. She will be paid less than a man doing comparable work because her main job is supposed to be taking care of her husband and children. She is part of a *reserve army of labor;* she can be hired when the economy can use her labor and fired when she is no longer needed by her employer, even if she would like to continue to work and her family could use extra income. Housewives are thus a flexible source of cheap labor in industrial societies.

Work in the marketplace and work in the home are inextricably intertwined. Because a woman rarely makes enough money to support herself and her children in capitalist economies, marriage is an economic necessity. A wife earns her husband's economic support by doing housework and taking care of their children. Her work in the home is not only necessary to the physical and emotional well-being of her husband and children, it is also vital to the economy. Women's housework and child care makes it possible for men to go to work and children to go to school, where they learn to take their future place in society—as workers, bosses, or the wives of workers or bosses. Mothers reproduce the social values of their class by passing them on to their children, teaching future bosses to be independent and take initiative and future workers and wives to be docile and obey orders.

A paper that was given at a workshop conference on occupational segregation at Wellesley College in 1975 was the start for what came to be known as *dual systems* theory in marxist feminism—an analysis of patriarchy and capitalism as twin systems of men's domination of women. The conference was mainstream and not at all marxist in its auspices—it was funded by the Carnegie Corporation and jointly sponsored by the American Economics Association Committee on the Status of Women and the Wellesley Center for Research on Women in Higher Education and the Professions. Yet the seed of a counter-theory to the liberal feminist view of gender inequality was planted there by Heidi Hartmann, an economist.

CAPITALISM AND PATRIARCHY

Heidi Hartmann

The present status of women in the labor market and the current arrangement of sex-segregated jobs is the result of a long process of interaction between patriarchy and capitalism. I have emphasized the actions of male workers throughout this process because I believe that emphasis to be correct. Men will have to be forced to give up their favored positions in the division of labor—in the labor market and at home—both if women's subordination is to end and if men are to begin to escape class oppression and exploitation. Capitalists have indeed used women as unskilled, underpaid labor to undercut male workers, yet this is only a case of the chickens coming home to roost—a case of men's cooptation by and support for patriarchal society, with its hierarchy among men, being turned back on themselves with a vengeance. Capitalism grew on top of patriarchy; patriarchal capitalism is stratified society par excellence. If nonruling-class men are to be free they will have to recognize their cooptation by patriarchal capitalism and relinquish their patriarchal benefits. If women are to be free, they must fight against both patriarchal power and capitalist organization of society.

Because both the sexual division of labor and male domination are so long standing, it will be very difficult to eradicate them and impossible to eradicate the latter without the former. The two are now so inextricably intertwined that it is necessary to eradicate the sexual division of labor itself in order to end male domination. Very basic changes at all levels of society and culture are required to liberate women. In this paper, I have argued that the maintenance of job segregation by sex is a key root of women's status, and I have relied on the operation of society-wide institutions to explain the maintenance of job segregation by sex. But the consequences of that division of labor go very deep, down to the level of the subconscious. The subconscious influences behavior patterns, which form the micro underpinnings (or complements) of social institutions and are in turn reinforced by those social institutions.

I believe we need to investigate these micro phenomena as well as the macro ones I have discussed in this paper. For example, it appears to be a very deeply ingrained behavioral rule that men cannot be subordinate to women of a similar social class. Manifestations of this rule have been noted in restaurants, where waitresses experience difficulty in giving orders to bartenders, unless the bartender can reorganize the situation to allow himself autonomy; among executives, where women executives are seen to be most successful if they have little contact with others at their level and manage small staffs; and among industrial workers, where female factory inspectors cannot successfully correct the work of male production workers. There is also a deeply ingrained fear of being identified with the other sex. As a general rule, men and women must never do anything which is not masculine or feminine (respectively). Male executives, for example, often exchange handshakes with male secretaries, a show of respect which probably works to help preserve their masculinity.

At the next deeper level, we must study the subconscious—both how these behavioral rules are internalized and how they grow out of personality structures. At this level, the formation of personality, there have been several attempts to study the production of gender, the socially imposed differentiation of humans based on biological sex differences. A materialist interpretation of reality, of course, suggests that gender production grows out of the extant division of labor between the sexes, and, in a dialectical process, reinforces that very division of labor itself. In my view, because of these deep ramifications of the sexual division of labor we will not eradicate sex-ordered task division until we eradicate the socially imposed gender differences between us and, therefore, the very sexual division of labor itself.

In attacking both patriarchy and capitalism we will have to find ways to change both society-wide institutions and our most deeply ingrained habits. It will be a long, hard struggle.

Reprinted from: Heidi Hartmann, "Capitalism, Patriarchy, and Job Segregation by Sex," in *Signs* 1(3, Pt.2):pp. 167–69. Copyright © 1976 by the University of Chicago Press. Reprinted by permission.

Marxist feminism once proposed that all women should get paid for housework and childcare; they should not do it for love alone. If wives were waged workers, they would be part of the gross national product and could get raises and vacations and sick leave. But there is a sense in which wives *are* paid for their work for the family; husbands supposedly are paid enough to maintain their families as well as themselves—they are supposed get what is called a *family wage*. The problem is that when a husband "pays" his wife for work in the home, either directly or indirectly, she is an economic dependent with few financial resources, a dangerous situation should her husband get sick, die, or leave her. The marxist and socialist feminist solution, like that of liberal feminism, is that women, too, should have permanent, full-time jobs. They would have independent means to fall back on in case they got a divorce or became a widow—or they did not have to get married at all, since they would be economically independent. For a mother, this solution needs affordable and accessible childcare services.

And what about people living in areas where neither women nor men can get jobs? Since the men in their communities are equally poor, women do not have an economic advantage in marrying. They have to rely on government support—what we call "welfare." In the United States, government welfare benefits go only to poor women (after a means test), and so these benefits—and the women who receive them— are singled out as deviant and stigmatized. In many industrialized countries, there is government financial support for all mothers, and benefits are much more extensive than in the United States. The benefits include prenatal care, paid maternal leave, maternal and child health services, cash allowances each month for each child, free education through college (including books), and childcare services. Every mother in the Scandinavian and other European countries and Israel receives some or most of these benefits. These *welfare states* recognize that producing children is work and that mothers therefore deserve state support. Their governments do not distinguish among poor and middle-class or wealthy women, or among full-time employees, part-time workers, and full-time homemakers. These services make it possible for all women to be both mothers and economically independent.

Such state welfare benefits were the norm in the former communist countries, but feminists there soon recognized that this solution to gender inequality only substitutes economic dependence on the state for dependence on a husband. Women are even more responsible for childcare, since the benefits are usually for the mother and rarely for the father. (Even when it is offered to them, few fathers take advantage of paid childcare leave.) Furthermore, when women take paid jobs, it is other women who still do the childcare, as paid workers in the home or in a childcare facility, or as unpaid "helpers." The women who do paid domestic labor in people's homes are usually from disadvantaged social groups; under capitalism, their wages tend to be minimal, and they rarely get any sick leave or health insurance, but in socialist countries, they get what any other worker receives.

The solution to women's economic dependence on men cannot simply be work for wages, if jobs continue to be gender-segregated and women's work is paid less than men's. Socialist feminism has a different solution to the gendered workforce than liberal feminism's program of affirmative action. It is *comparable worth.*

In examining the reasons why salaries for women and men are so discrepant, proponents of comparable worth found that wage scales are not set by the market for labor, or by what a worker is worth to an employer, or by the worker's education or other credentials. Salaries are set by conventional ideas of what men's and women's work is worth, which are rooted in sexism, racism, and other forms of discrimination. Comparable worth programs compare jobs in traditional women's occupations, such as secretary, with traditional men's jobs, such as automobile mechanic. They give point values for qualifications needed, skills used, extent of responsibility and authority over other workers, and dangerousness. Salaries are then equalized for jobs with a similar number of points (which represent the "worth" of the job). Although comparable worth programs do not do away with gendered job segregation, feminist proponents argue that raising the salaries of women doing traditional women's jobs could give the majority of women economic resources that would make them less dependent on marriage or state benefits as a means of survival.

The pros and cons of comparable worth are carefully weighed in the following overview by Roslyn Feldberg, a sociologist, presented at a conference of the International Working Group on Women and the Transformation of the Welfare State, held in Italy in 1983.

Comparable Worth

Roslyn L. Feldberg

. . . Comparable worth is related to the status quo in both the overall degree of inequality in the society and the hierarchy of wages. It can have only a modest effect on the overall degree of inequality because it does not attack all forms of inequality. It does attack gender inequality in the wage system, which is, as the earnings gap shows, a major component of gender inequality in the United States. The possibility that other forms of inequality will become more visible (e.g., similar patterns of wage differentials by race or age or inequities arising from the distribution of wealth) as a result of a lessening of gender inequality is not an argument against working for comparable worth. Indeed, struggles for comparable worth may set the stage for attacks on other forms of inequity.

How comparable worth will affect the hierarchy of wages is more difficult to foresee. On the one hand, it does not directly challenge the concept of a hierarchy; in fact, its insistence that jobs be evaluated implies a hierarchy. On the other hand, its rejection of the market as an adequate basis for determining wages initiates a discussion of how value is assigned to jobs independent of the market and which job dimensions are worthy of compensation. Advocates of comparable worth have challenged prevailing standards of evaluation. They have pointed out that formal job evaluations were first developed in industrial settings and tend to give considerable weight to tasks such as heavy lifting and the operation of expensive equipment. As a corollary, the skills and knowledge more typical of women's work are often unacknowledged or less heavily weighted. . . .

While comparable-worth advocates eschew questioning the principle of a hierarchy of wages, arguing only that they seek more objective, less sex-biased measures of job worth, the issues they raise provoke a broader debate. This debate does not . . . concern the feasibility of setting and applying such standards. Employers have been engaging in that activity for centuries. Rather the debate is about social values and priorities underlying the wage hierarchy. Is the labor-intensive work of caring for people less valuable than the work of caring for buildings or cars? How large a wage difference is reasonable between positions in the hierarchy? Or, to put it differently, what ought to be the relationship between wages and position in the job-evaluation hierarchy? What is the value of labor, and what social considerations ought to guide decisions about wages? These fundamental questions reveal how priorities are embedded in the market, where historical conventions and social and political, as opposed to purely economic, forces enter the process of setting wages.

The major legal questions concern the definition of discrimination and its relationship to established employment practices. Where these practices are long-standing, they are often seen by judges as well as by employers as arising naturally from economic laws or from differences among groups of workers. This perspective masks discrimination and creates difficulties for women who bring charges of unfair wages. The conflict is highlighted in both *Christensen v. State of Iowa* and *Lemons v. City and County of Denver*. In the former, the University of Northern Iowa was paying its secretaries less than its physical plant employees, although the university's own internal job evaluation awarded both categories the same labor grades. The Eighth Circuit Court ruled that these differences in pay were not evidence of discrimination because they reflected prevailing wage rates in the local labor market. Such legal opinions imbue the operating principles of the economic system with the force of natural law.

Comparable-worth advocates argue that the market is a historic development rather than an expression of natural law. Conventions within the market, including wage-setting practices and labor market divisions, perpetuate a historic discrimination against women and women's work. Without contesting the principle of hierarchy in wages, they advance the notion that wage hierarchies for women can be categorically lower than those for men only because they are discriminatory.

If comparable worth does succeed in raising women's wages, how will it affect relationships among groups of women and between women and men? Will it further divide women, stringing them out along the same hierarchy that divides male workers? If so, will it reduce our common ground and create new barriers to collective action?

First, all women should not continue to suffer from certain inequities simply because the proposed solution will not eliminate all inequities. Second, having said that, I believe it is crucial that we guard against further divisions both as a matter of simple justice and to prevent the gains from being eroded. The whole strength of the comparable-worth approach rests on cooperation among women. As long as some areas of women's paid work are devalued, the potential exists for all women's work to be devalued; consider the way in which arguments about married women not needing a living wage have been used against all women. Third, comparable worth can further divide women where they are already divided into separate occupational categories. For example, insofar as registered nurses tend to be white women and licensed practical nurses and nurses' aides tend to be women of color, comparable-worth attacks on inequities in nurses' wages could perpetuate and exacerbate divisions. There is no abstract, general solution for this potential problem. To the extent that the occupational distribution of white women and women of color has become more similar in the post-World War II period, the possibility is lessened. However, such structural shifts cannot eliminate the problem altogether. Divisions will be contained only by careful political analysis and concerted action. In the above example, the use of comparable worth to attack inequities based on gender provides the opportunity to develop conceptual and political tools that can also be used to address racial inequities among women. If gender-based inequities are eliminated between nurses and, for example, pharmacists, the same reasoning should be useful in attacking inequities between nurses and aides. That is not to say that comparable worth will create an egalitarian wage structure, but it will provide the grounds for eliminating wage inequities between groups doing comparable work.

A related concern is that comparable worth will become a class-specific strategy—advantageous to college-educated women at the expense of their high school counterparts and the latters' husbands. Again, such outcomes are possible, but there is already evidence that they are not necessary. . . .

Women who are not members of professional associations or unions will have less access to comparable-worth strategy than will those who are. Organized workers have an advantage in using methods that require major resources. This suggests that women need to do more organizing, with the support of unions and other sympathizers, not that comparable-worth strategy should be discounted.

The last question concerns relationships between men and women. Would comparable worth be disadvantageous for men? Would attempts to implement comparable worth lead to a new form of gender politics? Comparable worth could be relatively disadvantageous to men who are paid more than the content of their jobs warrants. No one has predicted absolute reductions in wages. Instead, the wages for these men's work would rise more slowly. Any attempt to lessen inequality would involve at least this form of disadvantage for some men.

Women married to those men might feel increased pressure to enter or remain in the labor force. Yet women's economic dependence on husbands' wages has proven insufficient for a large proportion of women. . . . In two-earner households, increases in women's wages would lessen the impact of a slower rise in men's wages, while they would improve the economic situation of the growing number of female-headed households.

The issue of gender politics is more problematic. There are already important divisions between men and women, which this article addresses. Economic self-sufficiency among women would radically alter the system of gender relations but would not necessarily exacerbate divisions. Materially, comparable worth is unlikely to work against the interests of most employed men. In fact, raising women's wages would probably raise the floor below men's wages, as the decline of a cheap labor supply in the past has bolstered wages. Furthermore, better-paid women workers would be in a stronger position to ally with men around common concerns. What comparable worth would threaten is the gender hierarchy in wages, which could be perceived as a threat to traditional notions of masculinity. Men's work and male workers would no longer automatically be seen as worth higher wages. Whether the new common standard would become a basis of solidarity or a loss of preeminence that men would fight depends in large part on the response of organized labor, especially at the local, grass-roots level.

Finally, I think that attempts to develop comparable worth claims would provide an opportunity for both organizing and consciousness raising. The history and dynamics of gender relations in the United States are such that women as well as men tend to devalue women's work. Many of us feel underpaid, yet few claim that we deserve men's wages. The few women who get such wages seem nervous, as if they occupy a position of privilege that is undeserved and might be taken away at any time. Given our experience of social subordination and low wages, it is not surprising that we are uncertain about the value of our work. The process of evaluating our own work and presenting claims on our own behalf might offer an opportunity to see our work more objectively, to appreciate its importance and its value.

In addition to its political program of comparable worth, socialist feminism expands the marxist feminist critique of the family as the source of women's oppression. Building on Marx's concept of *class consciousness*, which says that capitalists and members of the proletariat have conflicting interests and therefore an entirely different outlook on life, socialist feminism explores the ways that a wife's work in the home shapes her consciousness to be different from that of her husband. His work is future-oriented, geared to making a product or a profit; hers is present-oriented, getting dinner on the table and the children dressed for school every day. His work is abstract, dealing with money or ideas or an object; her work is hands-on, directly involved with living people who have bodily and emotional needs. He is supposed to be cool and impersonal and rational on the job; her job as wife and mother demands sensitivity to interpersonal cues and an outpouring of affection. He works as an individual, even when he brings home his paycheck; she is first and foremost a family member. In their ways of thinking and feeling, men and women are different kinds of people, not because their brains are wired differently but because their life experiences give them diverse consciousnesses.

The socialist feminist insight into women's "class consciousness," as we shall see, became the theoretical support for gender resistance feminisms.

Critique. Marxist and socialist feminisms have been the foundation of an influential economic theory of gender inequality that links the gendered division of labor in the family and in the workplace. The political solutions based on this theory, as carried out in the former communist countries and in democratic welfare states, improve women's material lives but fall far short of freeing women from men's control.

Marxist and socialist feminisms show that women are locked into a condition of lesser economic resources whether they are wives of workers or workers themselves. If they marry economically successful men, they become dependents, and if they marry poor men or not at all, they and their children can starve. The welfare-state solution—benefits to all mothers—is rooted in this analysis. There is, however, a negative side to state payments for childcare (the equivalent of wages for housework); they are important in giving mothers independent economic resources, but they can also keep women out of the paid marketplace or encourage part-time work. These policies thus have the latent function of keeping women a reserve army of cheap labor in capitalist, state-owned, and welfare-state economies.

Women's economic inequality in the family division of labor has been somewhat redressed in countries that give all mothers paid leave before and after the birth of a child and that provide affordable childcare. But that solution puts the burden of children totally on the mother and encourages men to opt out of family responsibilities altogether. (To counteract that trend, feminists in the government of Norway allocated a certain portion of paid childcare leave to fathers specifically.)

Women in the former communist countries had what liberal feminism in capitalist economies always wanted for women—full-time jobs with state-supported maternity leave and childcare services. But as marxist and socialist feminists recognize, the state can be as paternalistic as any husband. They argue that male-dominated government policies put the state's interests before those of women: When the economy needs workers, the state pays for childcare leave; with a downturn in the economy, the state reduces the benefits. Similarly, when the state needs women to have more children, it cuts back on availability of abortions and contraceptive services. Thus, the marxist and socialist feminist solution to women's economic inequality—full-time jobs and state-provided maternal and child welfare benefits—does not change women's status as primarily wives and mothers and men's status as the primary breadwinners. The gendered social order has been reformed but not significantly changed.

Summary

Marxist and socialist feminist theory emphasizes the economic and psychological differences between women and men, and men's power over women that emerges from their different statuses in the gendered division of labor. Marxist and socialist feminist theory is based on the division between work in the family (primarily women's work) and work in paid production (primarily men's work). Women are exploited because they work at production *and* reproduction in the home, and frequently at low-paying jobs outside the home as well.

In welfare-state economies that provide maternal and childcare benefits, a woman with children is better off materially than under capitalism, but she is not much more economically independent. Instead of the private patriarchy of economic dependence on a husband, women are subject to the public patriarchy of a paternalistic state, which is more interested in women as paid and unpaid workers and as child producers than in furthering gender equality in the home or in the workplace.

In all industrial economies, women and men have a different "class" consciousness because they do different work. Women have prime responsibility for childcare, even though they may work full time outside the home. Thus, they live a significant part of their lives in a world of reciprocity and cooperation, personal responsibility and sharing, physical contact and affection, in contrast to the impersonal and abstract world of industrial production, the world of men's work. Men's work in the marketplace is rewarded according to time spent or product made. Women's work in the home is never-ending; rewards depend on personalized standards, and others come first. It is emotional as well as intellectual and physical labor. Just as the economic positions of capitalists and the proletariat shape their class consciousness, women's daily material and socioemotional labor differentiates their consciousness from that of men.

Suggested Readings in Marxist and Socialist Feminism

Barrett, Michèle. 1988. *Women's Oppression Today: The Marxist/Feminist Encounter.* (Rev. ed.) London: Verso.

Coontz, Stephanie, and Peta Henderson. 1986. *Women's Work, Men's Property: The Origins of Gender and Class.* London: Verso.

Hansen, Karen V., and Ilene J. Phillipson (eds.). 1990. *Women, Class and the Feminist Imagination: A Socialist-Feminist Reader.* Philadelphia: Temple University Press.

Hartsock, Nancy C. M. 1983. *Money, Sex, and Power: Toward a Feminist Historical Materialism.* New York: Longman.

Hennessy, Rosemary. 1993. *Materialist Feminism and the Politics of Discourse.* London: Routledge.

Johnson, Kay Ann. 1983. *Women, the Family and Peasant Revolution in China.* Chicago: University of Chicago Press.

Sainsbury, Diane (ed.). 1994. *Gendering Welfare States.* Newbury Park, CA: Sage.

Sayers, Janet, Mary Evans, and Nanneke Redclift (eds.). 1987. *Engels Revisited: New Feminist Essays.* London and New York: Tavistock.

Stacey, Judith. 1983. *Patriarchy and Socialist Revolution in China.* Berkeley: University of California Press.

Stites, Richard. [1978] 1990. *The Women's Liberation Movement in Russia: Feminism, Nihilism, and Bolshevism, 1860–1930.* Princeton, NJ: Princeton University Press.

Walby, Sylvia. 1990. *Theorizing Patriarchy.* Oxford and New York: Basil Blackwell.

Chapter Three

Development Feminism

Sources of Gender Inequality

- Undercutting of women's traditional economic base by colonialism
- Exploitation of women workers in the post-colonial global economy
- Lack of education for girls
- Inadequate maternal and child health care
- Patriarchal family structures and cultural practices harmful to women and girls

Remedies

- Protection of women's economic resources in modernization programs
- Education of girls
- Health care and family planning services
- Community organizing of mothers
- Eradication of such practices as female genital mutilation[1]

Contributions

- Gender analyses of modernization and economic restructuring programs

- Data on exploitation of women and children workers
- Documentation of importance of economic resources to women's social status
- Recognition of women's rights as human rights

Economic exploitation of women in countries on the way to industrialization is even greater than in developed economies. Development feminist research has shown that women workers in developing countries in Latin America, the Caribbean, and Africa are paid less than men workers, whether they work in factories or do piece work at home. To survive in rural communities, women grow food, keep house, and earn money any way they can to supplement what their migrating husbands send them.

Development feminism uses theories of colonial underdevelopment and post-colonial development, as well as marxist and socialist feminist theories, to analyze the position of women in the global economy, with particular emphasis on newly industrializing countries. *The global economy* links countries whose economies focus on service, information, and finances with manufacturing sites and the sources of raw materials in other countries. Men and women workers all over the world supply the labor for the commodities that end up in the stores in your neighborhood. They are not paid according to their skills but according to the going wage, which varies enormously from country to country because it is dependent on the local standard of living. Women workers tend to be paid less than men workers throughout the world, whatever the wage scale, because they are supposedly supporting only themselves. However, in South Korea's economic development zone, many young single women factory workers live in crowded dormitories and eat one meal a day in order to send money home for a brother in college. In Mexico, many older married women's jobs are a significant source of their family's income.

The gendered division of labor in developing countries is the outcome of centuries of European and American colonization. Under colonialism, women's traditional contributions to food production were undermined in favor of exportable crops, such as coffee, and the extraction of raw materials, such as minerals. Men workers were favored in mining and large-scale agriculture, but they were barely paid enough for their own subsistence. Women family members had to provide food for themselves and their children; however, good land was often confiscated for plantations, so women also lived at a bare survival level.

Since becoming independent, many developing nations have sought financial capital and business investments from wealthier European and American countries. The consequent economic restructuring and industrialization disadvantages women. Men workers, considered heads of families, are hired for the better-paying manufacturing jobs. Young single women, although they are working as much for their families as for themselves, are hired for jobs that pay much less than men's jobs. And married women, whose wages frequently go to feed their children, are paid the least of all. For example, in the *maquiladoras*, the Mexican border industries, where 85 to 90 percent of the workers are women, there is a division between the electronics industries, which offer somewhat better working conditions and higher pay but hire only young single women, and the smaller, less modern apparel factories, which employ older women supporting children. In Puerto Rico's "Operation Bootstrap," a U.S.-sponsored economic development program of the 1950s, women were recruited into manufacturing industries that paid lower salaries than those where men workers predominated.

Feminist research on women's economic and health problems in developing countries has been extensive, but even those who work for government organizations, United Nations agencies, or the World Bank have not had the power to make development or economic restructuring programs more women-friendly. Pooling resources through grassroots organizing, women of different communities have joined together to fight against exploitation and for social services. They do so as mothers, for their children, and so have often been able to accomplish what more obvious political protest cannot, given the entrenchment of wealthy owners of land and factories.

The following excerpt is from a paper originally presented at an international conference, Women and Development: Focus on Latin America and Africa, sponsored by the Institute for Research on Women and the Center for Latin America and the Caribbean, which was held at the State University of New York at Albany in 1989. In it, Edna Acosta-Belén, a Latin American specialist, and Christine Bose, a sociologist, lay out feminist development theories dealing with the effects of colonialism, why poor women today are called "the last colony," and strategies of coping by these women.

GENDER AND DEVELOPMENT

Edna Acosta-Belén and Christine E. Bose

. . . It is difficult to address gender issues in the developing countries of Latin America and the Caribbean without recognizing that they are inextricably linked to a global capitalist and patriarchal model of accumulation and hence to the history of imperialist expansion and colonialism (Saffioti 1978; Mies et al. 1988). Although it is not always self-evident, both women and colonies have served as the foundations of industrial development of the economically dominant Western nations.

Colonialism, born in the fifteenth century—the gateway to discovery, exploration, and conquest—was to become the mainspring of European industrial development. Since the "discovery" of their existence by European settlers, primarily from Spain, Portugal, Great Britain, France, and the Netherlands, territories in the New World have served as the major sources of precious metals, labor, raw materials, and food products to support the commerce, consumption, and economic development of what are today's industrialized nations. The basis for the ascendancy of capitalism in Europe was the colonial exploitation of its overseas empires. Although the nature of colonization varied from one region of the world to another, the system was based on extracting the wealth of the new lands by using the labor of both the subjugated indigenous populations and that of the displaced and enslaved African populations to support the lavish lives of European aristocracies and the consumption needs of a rising bourgeoisie (Saffioti 1978; Etienne and Leacock 1980). The wealth and natural resources of the colonies were the essence of European mercantilist capitalism and, at a later stage, of its industrial revolution. The manufactured goods produced in European factories with the colonies' raw materials and labor found their way back into colonial markets. With some variations, this cycle has essentially perpetuated itself through the centuries.

In the Americas the United States emerged as a new colonial power to substitute for the Spanish, consolidating itself in the nineteenth century through the pursuit of its Manifest Destiny policies of territorial expansion and the Monroe Doctrine (1823), aimed at reducing European presence and influence in the hemisphere. After its Civil War

(1861-65) the United States was determined to become the major economic and geopolitical power in the Americas.

In the twentieth century capitalism entered its new monopoly and multinational stages of development, and the neocolonial relations developed then still link the colonizing and colonized countries into a global economic network. The unequal relationship that has kept Latin American and Caribbean nations dependent helps explain the continuing internal turmoil and clamor for change emanating from most of these nations today.

It is quite evident in the colonial literature that from the beginning of the European monarchies' imperial expansion, the adventurers, missionaries, and officials who came to the New World had little regard for any patterns of communal and egalitarian relationships among the native populations subjugated during the colonial enterprise. In many precolonial societies women's position and participation in productive activities was parallel to that of men, rather than subservient (Saffioti 1978; Etienne and Leacock 1980). The imposition of European patriarchal relationships that presupposed the universal subordination of women in many instances deprived indigenous women of property and personal autonomy and restricted the productive functions and any public roles they might have played before colonization (Saffioti 1978; Etienne and Leacock 1980; Nash 1980). These policies continued through the centuries as colonial territories were integrated into the capitalist system of production, and persisted even after those countries gained independence, in part because of the neocolonial relations the industrialized nations still maintain with developing countries. The conditions of *internal colonialism* (Blauner 1972) that later emerged within Western metropolitan centers, wherein immigrant groups and racial minorities are relegated to a structurally marginal position, replicate the patterns of colonial relationships.

Before the work of Ester Boserup (1970), most of the classical development literature tended to ignore women's economic role and contributions. Assuming women were passive dependents, the literature relegated them to reproductive rather than productive roles, confining them to an undervalued domestic sphere isolated from the rest of the social structure. Little attention was paid to differences in productivity between women and men in different developing nations or to women's labor activities in the informal economy. One of Boserup's major contributions was to establish empirically the vital role of women in agricultural economies and to recognize that economic development, with its tendency to encourage labor specialization, was actually depriving women of their original productive functions and on the whole deteriorating their status. . . .

Women as a Last Colony

The conceptualization of women as a last colony, advanced by the work of German feminist scholars Mies, Bennholdt-Thomsen, and Werlhof (1988), has provided a valuable new interpretative model for feminist research on Third World issues. This framework underscores the convergences of race, class, and gender and recognizes one complex but coherent system of oppression. It also allows us to see that the patterns of sexism are compounded by a layer of oppression, shared by Third World men and women, brought about by the colonizing experience.

Werlhof (1988, 25) argues that the relationship of Third World subsistence workers of both genders to First World multinationals in some ways resembles the relationship between men and women worldwide. Women and colonies are both low-wage and nonwage producers, share structural subordination and dependency, and are overwhelmingly poor. Werlhof contends that in response to its accumulation crisis, capitalism is now implicitly acknowledging that the unpaid labor of women in the household goes beyond the reproductive sphere into the production of commodities. Nevertheless, housewives are frequently and explicitly excluded from what is defined as the economy in order to maintain the illusion of the predominance of the male wage worker. The problems with this definition are increasingly obvious, as many Latin American and Caribbean households, using multiple income strategies, rely on women's informal economy activities or subsistence work. . . .

Mies et al. (1988,7) indicates there are actually three tiers in the capitalist pyramid of exploitation: (1) the holders of capital, (2) wage workers (mostly white men or the traditional proletariat) and nonwage workers (mostly women), and (3) housewives and subsistence producers (men and women) in the colonial countries. Using this model, both Werlhof (1988) and Bennholdt-Thomsen (1988) argue that the new international trend in the division of labor is toward the "housewifization" (*Hausfrauisierung*) of labor, namely, labor that exhibits the major characteristics of housework, and away from the classical proletariat whose labor is now being replaced. Of course, the housewife role entails different things across nations, ranging from cooking, cleaning, washing, and taking care of children and the elderly, to grinding maize, carrying water, or plowing the family plot. The determining factor is always whether or not these tasks are performed for wages. Werlhof (1988, 173) establishes a key link between the undervalued work performed by women and that of Third World populations, which leads her to conclude that the classical proletariat is being replaced by the Third World worker and the housewife as the new "pillars of accumulation." This conclusion also points to the contradiction between any cultural or economic devaluation of women's work and the important role it actually plays.

Following this line of argument, the three authors note that, since the latter part of the nineteenth century, patriarchal capitalist practice and ideology have colonized women by the "housewifization" of their work: by attempting to isolate women in the domestic sphere and devaluing the work they perform there; by ideologically justifying it as a genetic predisposition based on their capacity for motherhood; by regarding any type of income they generate as supplementary or secondary, thus ascribing a lower status to their occupations; and ultimately, by controlling their sexuality. These power relations between men and women are thus comparable to the international division of labor between First and Third World countries. The present-day world economic crisis is not just another cycle of capitalism but rather a new phase of development relying on female forms of labor (i.e., doing any kind of work at any time, unpaid or poorly paid) wherein the industrialized powers try to force Third World nations to "restructure" or adapt their national economies to the needs of the world system for such flexible labor. . . .

Women Organizing for Change

. . . Women are not passive victims in the socioeconomic processes that maintain their lower status. Instead, they are developing creative ways in which to resist the new forms of subordination. Latin American activists expect that changes in sexist practice and ideology can be obtained during economic crises—an experience quite different from that of feminists in the core capitalist countries whose achievements were made in the context of improving material conditions. In Latin America and the Caribbean various types of resistance, solidarity, and collective action are used by women in diverse geographic regions and under different sociopolitical structures, a pattern that is beginning to be recognized in comparative studies of women's movements (Margolis 1993).

Although Latin American women's subsistence activities as peasant producers can be seen as similar to the unpaid housework of women in Europe and the United States, the resultant political strategies are different . . . perhaps because of the class differences between them. In First World countries women have responded to cutbacks in government services to families by entering the paid labor force, especially in the service industry, and by taking over the tasks of eldercare and childcare. In Latin America and the Caribbean nations, though some women do create microenterprises, . . . take jobs in export processing zones, or enter the service sector, the vast majority respond to the breakdown of their subsistence economy by organizing collective meals, health cooperatives, mothers' clubs, neighborhood water-rights groups, or their own textile and craft collectives, which produce goods both for street vending and for international markets. Thus, rather than *privatizing* their survival problems, these women *collectivize* them and form social-change groups based on social reproduction concerns. In these new terms, the political discourse and arena of struggle is not worker exploitation and control of the means of production but rather moral persuasion to place demands on the state for rights related to family survival.

Many Latin American women activists contend that their traditional roles as wives and mothers are the basis for these collective actions on behalf of their families. Although most of the groups are composed of poor women, they do not organize either explicitly on a class basis or at the workplace. Instead, they organize at a neighborhood level around a broad list of issues that they redefine as women's concerns, such as running water or transportation for squatter communities. Some feminist scholars argue that this approach constitutes a movement of women but not necessarily a feminist movement; others feel these tactics represent a form of working-class feminism that promotes consciousness of how gender shapes women's lives (Sternback et al. 1992). . . .

References

Bennholdt-Thomsen, Veronika. 1988a. "'Investment of the Poor': An Analysis of World Bank Policy." In *Women: The Last Colony,* ed. Maria Mies, Veronika Bennholdt-Thomsen, and Claudia von Werlhof, 51–63. London: Zed.

Blauner, Robert. 1972. *Radical Oppression in America.* New York: Harper and Row.

Boserup, Ester. 1970. *Women's Role in Economic Development.* New York: St. Martin's Press.

Etienne, Mona, and Eleanor Leacock (eds.). 1980. *Women and Colonization: Anthropological Perspectives.* New York: Praeger.

Margolis, Diane Rothbard. 1993. "Women's Movements Around the World: Cross-Cultural Comparisons." *Gender & Society* 7: 379–99.

Mies, Maria, Veronika Bennholdt-Thomsen, and Claudia von Werlhof. 1988. *Women: The Last Colony.* London: Zed.

Nash, June. 1980. "Aztec Women: The Transition from Status to Class in Empire and Colony." In *Women and Colonization: Anthropological Perspectives,* pp. 134–48.

Saffioti, Heleieth I. B. 1978. *Women in Class Society.* New York: Monthly Review.

Sternback, Nancy Saporta, Marysa Navarro-Aranguren, Patricia Chuchryk, and Sonia E. Alvarez. 1992. "Feminisms in Latin America: From Bogotá to San Bernardo." *Signs* 17:393–434.

Werlhof, Claudia von. 1988a. "Women's Work: The Blind Spot in the Critique of Political Economy." In *Women: The Last Colony,* ed. Maria Mies, Veronika Bennholdt-Thomsen, and Claudia von Werlhof, 13–26. London: Zed.

Development feminism equates women's status with their contribution to their family's economy and their control of economic resources. To be equal with her husband, it is not enough for a married woman to earn money; she has to provide a needed portion of her family's income and also have control over the source of that income and over its distribution as well. In a rural community, that means owning a piece of land, being able to market the harvest from that land, and deciding how the profit from the sale will be spent. In an urban economy, it may mean owning a store or small business, retaining the profit, and deciding what to spend it on or whether to put it back into the business.

There are societies in Africa and elsewhere in the world where women control significant economic resources and so have a high status. In contrast, in societies with patriarchal family structures where anything women produce, including children, belongs to the husband, women and girls have a low value. Development feminism's theory is that in any society, if the food or income women produce is the main way the family is fed, and women also control the distribution of any surplus they produce, women have power and prestige. If men provide most of the food and distribute the surplus, women's status is low. Whether women or men produce most of the food or bring in most of the family income depends on the society's economy. When a woman is able to own the means of production (land, a store, a business) like a man, she has the chance to be economically independent. If her income is barely above subsistence level because her choices are low-waged work in a factory, piece work in a sweatshop, or sex work as a prostitute, then the fact that she has a job does not give her a very high social status, especially if much of the money she earns is sent back home to her family.

Thus, the mode of production and the kinship rules that control the distribution of any surplus are the significant determinants of the relative status of women and men in any society. In the following excerpt, Deniz Kandiyoti, a British sociologist, describes how women themselves recognize the importance of an economic base for their domestic bargaining power.

BARGAINING WITH PATRIARCHY

Deniz Kandiyoti

. . . I had one of my purest experiences of culture shock in the process of reviewing the literature on women in agricultural development projects in sub-Saharan Africa (Kandiyoti 1985). Accustomed as I was to only one type of patriarchy (. . . classic patriarchy), I was ill prepared for what I found. The literature was rife with instances of women's resistance to attempts to lower the value of their labor and, more important, women's refusal to allow the total appropriation of their production by their husbands. Let me give some examples.

Wherever new agricultural schemes provided men with inputs and credit, and the assumption was made that as heads of household they would have access to their wives' unremunerated labor, problems seemed to develop. In the Mwea irrigated rice settlement in Kenya, where women were deprived of access to their own plots, their lack of alternatives and their total lack of control over men's earnings made life so intolerable to them that wives commonly deserted their husbands (Hanger and Moris 1973). In Gambia, in yet another rice-growing scheme, the irrigated land and credit were made available only to men, even though it was the women who traditionally grew rice in tidal swamps, and there was a long-standing practice of men and women cultivating their own crops and controlling the produce. Women's customary duties with respect to labor allocation to common and individual plots protected them from demands by their husbands that they provide free labor on men's irrigated rice fields. Men had to pay their wives wages or lend them an irrigated plot to have access to their labor. In the rainy season, when women had the alternative of growing their own swamp rice, they created a labor bottleneck for the men, who simply had to wait for the days women did not go to their own fields. . . .

In short, the insecurities of African polygyny for women are matched by areas of relative autonomy, which they clearly strive to maximize. Men's responsibility for their wives' support, although normative in some instances, is in actual fact relatively low. Typically, it is the woman who is primarily responsible for her own and her children's upkeep, including meeting the costs of their education, with variable degrees of assistance from her husband. Women have very little to gain and a lot to lose by becoming totally dependent on husbands; hence they quite rightly resist projects that tilt the delicate balance they strive to maintain. In their protests, wives are safeguarding already existing spheres of autonomy. . . .

Works on historical transformations suggest that colonization eroded the material basis for women's relative autonomy (such as usufructuary access to communal land or traditional craft production) without offering attenuating modifications in either marketplace or marital options. The more contemporary development projects also tend to assume or impose a male-headed corporate family model, which curtails women's options without opening up other avenues to security and well-being. The women perceive these changes, especially if they occur abruptly, as infractions that constitute a breach of their existing accommodations with the order dominated by men. Consequently, they openly resist them.

References

Hanger, J. and J. Moris. 1973. "Women and the Household Economy." Pp. 209–44 in *Mwea: An Irrigated Rice Settlement in Kenya*, edited by R. Chambers and J. Moris. Munich: Weltforum Verlag.

Kandiyoti, D. 1985 *Women in Rural Production Systems: Problems and Policies*. Paris: UNESCO.

In addition to gendered economic analyses, development feminism addresses the political issue of women's rights versus national and cultural traditions. At the United Nations Fourth World Conference on Women and the NGO (nongovernmental organizations) Forum held in Beijing in 1995, the popular slogan was "human rights are women's rights and women's rights are human rights." The Platform for Action document that came out of the U.N. Conference condemned particular cultural practices that are oppressive to women—infanticide, dowry, child marriage, and female genital mutilation. The 187 governments that signed onto the Platform agreed to abolish these practices. However, since they are integral parts of cultural and tribal traditions, giving them up could be seen as kowtowing to Western ideas. The development feminist perspective, so critical of colonial and cultural imperialism and yet so supportive of women's rights, has found this issue difficult to resolve.

The women's own solution to this dilemma is community organizing around their productive and reproductive roles as mothers—so that what benefits them economically and physically is in the service of their families, not themselves alone. However, this same community organizing and family service can support the continuance of cultural practices, such as female genital mutilation, that Western development feminists want to see eradicated. The decision not to interfere with traditional cultural practices that are physically harmful to girls and at the same time work for the girls' education and better health care is a dilemma for development feminists.

Critique*.* Development feminism has taken marxist and socialist feminist theories and expanded their application to nonindustrial economies and to societies in the process of industrializing. They have found many of the same phenomena that occurred during the nineteenth-century European and American industrial revolution—young, single factory girls exploited as cheap labor, working-class men getting the better-paid factory jobs, and middle- and upper-class men owning the means of production. They also found that the family remains a source of both exploitation and protection for women. Their labor is frequently used as a source of family income, but mothers also form grassroots service and community protest groups.

Western ideas of individualism are double-edged in developing countries. On the one hand, these ideas support the rights of girls and women to an education that will allow them to be economically independent. They are also the source of a concept of universal human rights, which can be used to fight subordinating and sometimes physically hurtful tribal practices, such as female genital mutilation. On the other hand, Western ideas undercut communal enterprises and traditional sharing of food production and childcare.

Summary

The global economy reflects state and private economic interests, and that means high production with cheap labor for maximum profits. Families all over the world need several workers in order to survive, often including children. Women and girls are doubly vulnerable—as workers and as family members. They are a prime source of low-paid wage workers whose earnings belong first to their families. They also work in family businesses, often unpaid; they make things at home to sell to supplement their family's food supply; they become prostitutes at a young age, often sold as a source of family income. At the same time, women physically maintain households and have babies, and frequently bury them within a year of birth.

There is no doubt that in many parts of the world today, as development feminism has shown, women are living in dire conditions. To redress their situation, whole economic structures and family and kinship systems need to be overhauled. However, the twentieth-century economic and social revolutions in the Soviet Union and China did not give women equality. Women became fulltime workers, but, as in capitalist economies, they earned less than men and did almost all the child care and housework.

Development feminism makes very evident the political dilemmas of gender reform feminisms. Throughout the world, men own most of the private property, monopolize the better jobs, and make the laws.

The outcome of this inequality is men's double exploitation of women in the job market and in the home. Procreative differences are not the cause of women's exploitation, but its justification. Women are subordinate in all industrial societies not because they are child bearers or child minders but because economies depend on them as low-paid workers who can be hired and fired as needed. The rationale is that women are, after all, "really" wives and mothers. Each form of exploitation of women's work reinforces the other. Women's economic value as waged and low-waged workers and as unpaid workers for the family are the *main* reasons for their subordination in modern societies.

Gender reform feminist politics is correct in pinpointing women's position in the world of paid work as the target for change. The problem is that the entire global economy needs drastic change. If the global economy is not made more equal for everyone, women in general, and poor women in particular, suffer the most. But since the gendered social order as a whole is the source of gender inequality, economic changes alone will not necessarily put women on an equal footing with men.

Note

1. For more than two thousand years, in a broad belt across the middle of Africa, little girls and young women have been subject to crude surgery that cuts away the clitoris and the lips of the vagina. The vaginal opening is sewn closed, except for a tiny opening for urination and menstruation. The purpose is to ensure women's virginity until marriage and to inhibit wives' appetites for sexual relations after marriage. Ironically, these mutilating practices do neither but result in the infliction of pain and the practice of anal intercourse as part of normal sexuality. Childbirth is more dangerous because of tearing and hemorrhage, and the risks of abscesses, fistulas, and urinary tract infection throughout life are high.

Suggested Readings in Development Feminism

Boserup, Ester. 1970. [second edition, 1987]. *Women's Role in Economic Development*. New York: St. Martin's Press.

El Dareer, Asma. 1982. *Woman, Why Do You Weep? Circumcision and Its Consequences*. London: Zed Books.

Kim, Seung-Kyung. 1997. *Class Struggle or Family Struggle? The Lives of Women Factory Workers in South Korea*. Cambridge, UK: Cambridge University Press.

Mies, Marie. 1986. *Patriarchy and Accumulation on a World Scale.* London: Zed Books.

Mies, Maria, Veronika Bennholdt-Thomsen, and Claudia von Werlhof. 1988. *Women: The Last Colony.* London: Zed Books.

Moghadam, Valentine M. (ed.). 1994. *Identity Politics and Women: Cultural Reassertions and Feminisms in International Perspective.* Boulder, CO: Westview Press.

——. (ed.). 1996. *Patriarchy and Development: Women's Positions at the End of the Twentieth Century.* Oxford, UK: Clarendon Press.

Nash, June, and María Patricia Fernández-Kelly (eds.). 1983. *Women, Men, and the International Division of Labor.* Albany: State University of New York Press.

Redclift, Nanneke, and M. Thea Stewart (eds.). 1991. *Working Women: International Perspectives on Women and Gender Ideology.* New York and London: Routledge.

Scheper-Hughes, Nancy. 1992. *Death Without Weeping: The Violence of Everyday Life in Brazil.* Berkeley: University of California Press.

Sparr, Pam (ed.). 1994. *Mortgaging Women's Lives: Feminist Critiques of Structural Adjustment.* London: Zed Books.

Ward, Kathryn. (ed.). 1990. *Women Workers and Global Restructuring.* Ithaca, NY: ILR Books.

Young, Kate, Carol Wolkowitz, and Roslyn McCullagh (eds.). 1981. *Of Marriage and the Market: Women's Subordination in International Perspective.* London: CSE Books.

Part III

GENDER RESISTANCE FEMINISMS

Overview

In the 1970s, feminist ideas began to make inroads into the public consciousness, and women entered many formerly all-men workplaces and schools. Derogatory remarks about women were no longer acceptable officially, but women became more and more aware of constant put-downs from men they saw every day—bosses and colleagues at work, professors and students in the classroom, fellow organizers in political movements, and worst of all, from boyfriends and husbands at home. These "microinequities" of everyday life—being ignored and interrupted, not getting credit for competence or good performance, being passed over for jobs that involve taking charge—crystallize into a pattern that insidiously wears women down. Mary Rowe, a woman doctor using a pseudonym (because it was too dangerous even in the late 1970s to openly call attention to what men colleagues were doing to women), termed it the "Saturn's Rings Phenomenon" at a Conference on Women's Leadership and Authority in the Health Professions, held in California in 1977. The seemingly trivial sexist incidents, she said, are like the dust particles in the rings around the planet Saturn—separately they are tiny, but when they coalesce, they form a very visible pattern.

The younger women working in the civil rights, anti-Vietnam War, and student new-left movements in the late 1960s had even earlier realized that they were being used as handmaidens, bed partners, and coffee-makers by the men in their protest organizations. Despite the revolutionary rhetoric the young men were flinging in the face of Western civilization in many countries, when it came to women, they might as well have been living in the eighteenth century.

Out of this awareness that sisters had no place in any brotherhood came the American and European gender resistance feminisms. Their watchword is *patriarchy*, or men's subordination of women. Gender resistance feminisms argue that patriarchy can be found wherever women and men are in contact with each other, in public life as well as in the family. It is very hard to eradicate because a sense of their superiority to women is deeply embedded in the consciousness of most men and is built into the structures of Western society. It can best be resisted by forming nonhierarchical, supportive, woman-only organizations, where women can think and act and create free of constant sexist put-downs.

Radical feminism is characterized by small, leaderless, women-only consciousness-raising groups, where the topics of intense discussion come out of the commonalities of women's lives—housework, emotional and sexual service to men, menstruation, childbirth, menopause, the constant sexual innuendoes and come-ons in workplaces and on college campuses, the lack of control over procreation. Politically, radical feminism took on the violence in women's oppression—rape and wife beating, the depiction of women as sex objects in the mass media and as pieces of meat in pornography, the global commerce in prostitution. This sexual exploitation of women is the worst effect of patriarchy, according to radical feminism, because its goal is social control of all women. Even if they are not directly attacked, the threat can be enough to keep women fearful and timid.

Lesbian feminism argues that sexual violence and exploitation are the common downside of romantic heterosexual love, which itself is oppressive to women. Lesbian feminists are active in women-only political activities, such as Take Back the Night marches, and in cultural events, such as women-only festivals, as well as in women-run businesses.

Psychoanalytic feminism provides the theory of why men oppress women. Using Freudian concepts of personality development, psychoanalytic feminism argues that men's fear of castration by their mothers and repression of their primal attachment to her is sublimated in a *phallic* (sexual male) culture that symbolically subordinates and controls women. Politically, French feminism counters with cultural productions, particularly literature, that celebrate women's bodies, sexuality, and maternality.

Standpoint feminism brought all these feminist theories and politics together in a research agenda: Not only culture but science and social science have to formulate questions and gather data from a *woman's standpoint*. The heady possibilities of creating theory, knowledge, and art out of women's experiences forges the bonds of sisterhood and the rationale for separation from men.

The important theoretical contribution of gender resistance feminisms has been in showing that women's devaluation and subordination are part of the ideology and values of Western culture, as represented in religion, the mass media, sports, and cultural productions, and are built into the everyday practices of major institutions, such as medicine, the law, science, and social science. They also show how sexual exploitation and violence, especially rape and pornography, are a means of control of women.

Some political remedies—women-only consciousness-raising groups, alternative organizations, and lesbian separatism—are resistant to the gendered social order, but they are not able to transform it, as they stand apart from mainstream social institutions. They are vital in allowing women the "breathing space" to formulate important theories of gender inequality, to develop women's studies programs in colleges and universities, to form communities, and to produce knowledge, culture, ethics, and religions from a woman's point of view. But they alienate heterosexual White working-class women and women of disadvantaged racial or ethnic groups, who feel that their men are just as oppressed as they are by the dominant society. These women would not desert their brothers for a sisterhood they feel does not welcome them anyway.

More effective have been the feminist campaigns against sexual harassment, rape, battering, incest, pornography, and prostitution. They have, however, led to head-on confrontations with some men's sense of sexual entitlement and have produced considerable anti-feminist backlash.

Chapter Four

Radical Feminism

Sources of Gender Inequality

- A system of men's oppression of women (*patriarchy*) that goes beyond discrimination
- Men's violence and control of women through rape, battering, and murder
- Legitimation of women's oppression in law, medicine, religion, and other social institutions
- Objectification of women's bodies in advertisements, mass media, and cultural productions
- Sexual exploitation in pornography and prostitution

Remedies

- More effective laws against rape and battering
- Rape crisis centers and battered women's shelters
- Take Back the Night marches
- Identification of sexual harassment as a form of discrimination
- Praise for all kinds of women's bodies, women's sexuality, and maternal qualities

Contributions

- Theory of patriarchy as a system of oppression of women

- Recognition of violence against women as a means of direct and indirect control
- Getting stronger legislation against rape and battering
- Establishment of accessible rape crisis centers and battered women's shelters
- Sexual harassment guidelines for workplaces and schools
- Making evident the dangers of date rape
- Women's studies programs in colleges and universities throughout the world

The 1970s saw the growth of what has become a major branch of feminism. Originally used as a term for feminists who wanted to do away with the traditional family and motherhood, radical feminism became a perspective that makes motherhood into a valuable way of thinking and behaving. However, it continues to criticize the traditional family as a prime source of patriarchal oppression of women, as does marxist feminism.

Radical feminism expands the concept of *patriarchy* by defining it as a world-wide system of subordination of women by men through violence and sexual exploitation. In the radical feminist view, because of Western society's encouragement of aggressiveness in men and sexual display in women, most men are capable of, if not prone to, violence against women, and most women are potential victims. The constant threat of rape, battering, and murder is a powerful means of keeping women "in their place." Movies, TV, and advertisements in all media sexualize women's bodies. The pervasive sexual objectification encourages men's using women for their own needs. Also, if women are depicted as "sex objects," their intellectual and leadership capabilities disappear from view. Women running for political office have to look attractive but dare not look too sexy.

Sexual harassment is the commonest manifestation of the sexual exploitation of women in Western societies: Unwanted sexual invitations, sexually loaded remarks and jokes, and inappropriate comments on dress or appearance make it difficult for women and girls to do their work (or even to walk down the street unmolested). When the response to a work-related request is, "Wow, that sweater really brings out your good points," the not-so-subtle intent is to turn a woman colleague into a "bimbo" and take her out of the running as a serious competitor. More obvious sexual harassment occurs when a boss or teacher threatens the loss of a job or a low grade if a worker or student will not "give a kiss" or if she responds to a grope with a slap. In the military and other hierarchical organizations, women feel that reporting a rape or coerced sex, let alone a pattern of demeaning comments, is useless when the higher-ups have the same sexist attitudes. Women who complain get tainted with a "troublemaker" label, or are harassed by the person they complain to, but their harassers are let off with a mild talking-to. Sexual harassment seems to get attention only when the media report a drunken attack on many women in a public place, or the same situation is found in army base after army base, or a high government official is involved.

When sexual harassment adversely affects a worker's or student's appointment or evaluation, or the environment in which they work or study, it becomes a form of discrimination. Radical feminism has made these patterns of sexual harassment and their discriminatory results visible. Its analysis is reflected in the sexual harassment guidelines of many schools and workplaces. In these guidelines, a sexual involvement of any kind between a subordinate and a person in a position of power is considered coercive and is explicitly forbidden. Also actionable is any situation where sexual remarks or uninvited attentions make employees or students so uncomfortable that they are unable to concentrate on work. These guidelines set up formal processes for reports and complaints and rules for actions to be taken in cases of proven sexual harassment.

Although radical feminism's political battlefield has been protection of rape victims and battered women and condemnation of pornography, prostitution, and sexual harassment, some writers have blamed the unequal power in heterosexual relationships for being oppressive to women. They argue that since all men derive power from their dominant social status, any sexual relationship between women and men takes place in a socially unequal context. Consent by women to heterosexual intercourse is, by this definition, often forced by emotional appeals and threats to end the relationship. When a woman fears that a date or friend or lover or husband will use physical violence if she does not give in, it is *date rape* or *marital rape*, and is as abusive as any other kind of rape.

The following excerpt is by Catharine MacKinnon, a feminist lawyer whose theoretical and legal arguments that sexuality and violence form a continuum of oppression have become the foundation for radical feminism. It was developed for the National Conference on Women and the Law, which met in Boston in 1981.

Sex and Violence

Catharine A. MacKinnon

I want to raise some questions about the concept of this panel's title, "Violence against Women," as a concept that may coopt us as we attempt to formulate our own truths. I want to speak specifically about four issues: rape, sexual harassment, pornography, and battery. I think one of the reasons we say that each of these issues is an example of violence against women is to reunify them. To say that aggression against women has this unity is to criticize the divisions that have been imposed on that aggression by the legal system. What I see to be the danger of the analysis, what makes it potentially cooptive, is formulating it—and it *is* formulated this way—these are issues of violence, *not* sex: rape is a crime of violence, not sexuality; sexual harassment is an abuse of power, not sexuality; pornography is violence against women, it is not erotic. Although battering is not categorized so explicitly, it is usually treated as though there is nothing sexual about a man beating up a woman so long as it is with his fist. I'd like to raise some questions about that as well.

I hear in the formulation that these issues are violence against women, not sex, that we are in the shadow of Freud, intimidated at being called repressive Victorians. We're saying we're *op*pressed and they say we're *re*pressed. That is, when we say we're against rape, the immediate response is, "Does that mean you're against sex?" "Are you attempting to impose neo-Victorian prudery on sexual expression?" This comes up with sexual harassment as well. When we say we're against sexual harassment, the first thing people want to know is, "What's the difference between that and ordinary male-to-female sexual initiation?" That's a good question. . . . The same is also true of criticizing pornography. "You can't be against erotica?" It's the latest version of the accusation that feminists are anti-male. To distinguish ourselves from this, and in reaction to it, we call these abuses violence. The attempt is to avoid the critique—we're not against sex—and at the same time retain our criticism of these practices. So we rename as violent those abuses that have been seen to be sexual, without saying that we have a very different perspective on violence and on sexuality and their relationship. I also think a reason we call these experiences violence is to avoid being called lesbians, which for some reason is equated with being against sex. In order to avoid that, yet retain our opposition to sexual violation, we put this neutral, objective, abstract word *violence* on it all.

To me this is an attempt to have our own perspective on these outrages without owning up to having one. To have our point of view but present it as *not* a particular point of view. Our problem has been to label something as rape, as sexual harassment, as pornography in the face of a suspicion that it might be intercourse, it might be ordinary sexual initiation, it might be erotic. To say that these purportedly sexual events violate us, to be against them, we call them not sexual. But the attempt to be objective and neutral avoids owning up to the fact that women do have a specific point of view on these events. It avoids saying that from women's point of view, intercourse, sex roles, and eroticism can be and at times are violent to us as women.

My approach would claim our perspective; we are not attempting to be objective about it, we're attempting to represent the point of view of women. The point of view of men up to this time, called objective, has been to distinguish sharply between rape on the one hand and intercourse on the other; sexual harassment on the one hand and normal, ordinary sexual initiation on the other; pornography or obscenity on the one hand and eroticism on the other. The male point of view defines them by distinction. What women experience does not so clearly distinguish the normal, everyday things from those abuses from which they have been defined by distinction. Not just "Now we're going to take what *you* say is rape and call it violence"; "Now we're going to take what *you* say is sexual harassment and call it violence"; "Now we're going to take what *you* say is pornography and call it violence." We have a deeper critique of what has been done to women's sexuality and who controls access to it. What we are saying is that sexuality in exactly these normal forms often *does* violate us. So long as we say that those things are abuses of violence, not sex, we fail to criticize what has been made of *sex,* what has been done to us *through* sex, because we leave the line between rape and intercourse, sexual harassment and sex roles, pornography and eroticism, right where it is.

I think it is useful to inquire how women and men (I don't use the term *persons,* I guess, because I haven't seen many lately) live through the meaning of their experience with these issues. When we ask whether rape, sexual harassment, and pornography are questions of violence or questions of sexuality, it helps to ask, to whom? What is the perspective of those who are involved, whose experience it is—to rape or to have been raped, to consume pornography or to be consumed through it. As to what these things *mean* socially, it is important whether they are about sexuality to women and men or whether they are instead about "violence,"—or whether violence and sexuality can be distinguished in that way, as they are lived out.

The crime of rape—this is a legal and observed, not a subjective, individual, or feminist definition—is defined around penetration. That seems to me a very male point of view on what it means to be sexually violated. And it is exactly what heterosexuality as a social institution is fixated around, the penetration of the penis into the vagina. Rape is defined according to what men think violates women, and that is the same as what they think of as the *sine qua non* of sex. What women experience as degrading and defiling when we are raped includes as much that is distinctive to us as is our experience of sex. Someone once termed penetration a "peculiarly resented aspect" of rape—I don't know whether that meant it was peculiar that it was resented or that it was resented with heightened peculiarity. Women who have been raped often do resent having been penetrated. But that is not all there is to what was intrusive or expropriative of a woman's sexual wholeness.

I do think the crime of rape focuses more centrally on what men define as sexuality than on women's experience of our sexual being, hence its violation. A common experience of rape victims is to be unable to feel good about anything heterosexual thereafter—or anything sexual at all, or men at all. The minute they start to have sexual feelings or feel sexually touched by a man, or even a woman, they start to relive the rape. I had a client who came in with her husband. She was a rape victim, a woman we had represented as a witness. Her husband sat the whole time and sobbed. They couldn't have sex anymore because every time he started to touch her, she would flash to the rape scene and see his face change into the face of the man who had raped her. That, to me, is sexual. When a woman has been raped, and it is sex that she then cannot experience without connecting it to that, it was her sexuality that was violated.

Similarly, men who are in prison for rape think it's the dumbest thing that ever happened. . . . It isn't just a miscarriage of justice; they were put in jail for something very little different from what most men do most of the time and call it sex. The only difference is they got caught. That view is nonremorseful and not rehabilitative. It may also be true. It seems to me we have here a convergence between the rapist's view of what he has done and the victim's perspective on what was done to her. That is, for both, their ordinary experiences of heterosexual intercourse and the act of rape have something in common. Now this gets us into intense trouble, because that's exactly how judges and juries see it who refuse to convict men accused of rape. A rape victim has to prove that it was not intercourse. She has to show that there was force and she resisted, because if there was sex, consent is inferred. Finders of fact look for "more force than usual during the preliminaries." Rape is defined by distinction from intercourse—not nonviolence, intercourse. They ask, does this event look more like fucking or like rape? But what is their standard for sex, and is this question asked from the *woman's point of view?* The level of force is not adjudicated at her point of violation; it is adjudicated at the standard of the normal level of force. Who sets this standard?

In the criminal law, we can't put everybody in jail who does an ordinary act, right? Crime is supposed to be deviant, not normal. Women continue not to report rape, and a reason is that they believe, and they are right, that the legal system will not see it from their point of view. We get very low conviction rates for rape. We also get many women who believe they have never been raped, although a lot of force was involved. They mean that they were not raped in a way that is legally provable. In other words, in all these situations, there was not *enough* violence against them to take it beyond the category of "sex"; they were not coerced enough. Maybe they were forced-fucked for years and put up with it, maybe they tried to get it over with, maybe they were coerced by something other than battery, something like economics, maybe even something like love.

What I am saying is that unless you make the point that there is much violence in intercourse, as a usual matter, none of that is changed. Also we continue to stigmatize the women who claim rape as having experienced a deviant violation and allow the rest of us to go through life feeling violated but thinking we've never been raped, when there were a great many times when we, too, have had sex and didn't want it. What this critique does that is different from the "violence, not sex" critique is ask a series of questions about normal, heterosexual intercourse and attempt to move the line between heterosexuality on the one hand—intercourse—and rape on the other, rather than allow it to stay where it is.

Having done that so extensively with rape, I can consider sexual harassment more briefly. The way the analysis of sexual harassment is sometimes expressed now (and it bothers me) is that it is an abuse of power, not sexuality. That does not allow us to pursue whether sexuality, as socially constructed in our society through gender roles, is *itself* a power structure. If you look at sexual harassment as power, not sex, what is power supposed to be? Power is employer/employee, not because courts are marxist but because this is a recognized hierarchy. Among men. Power is teacher/student, because courts recognize a hierarchy there. Power is on one side and sexuality on the other. Sexuality is ordinary affection, everyday flirtation. Only when ordinary, everyday affection and flirtation and "I was just trying to be friendly" come into the context of *another* hierarchy is it considered potentially an abuse of power. What is not considered to be a hierarchy is women and men—men on top and women on the bottom. That is not considered to be a question of power or social hierarchy, legally or politically. A feminist perspective suggests that it is.

When we have examples of coequal sexual harassment (within these other hierarchies), worker to worker on the same level, involving women and men, we have a lot of very interesting, difficult questions about sex discrimination, which is supposed to be about gender difference, but does not conceive of gender as a social hierarchy. I think that implicit in race discrimination cases for a brief moment of light was the notion that there is a social hierarchy between Blacks and whites. So that presumptively it's an exercise of power for a white person to do something egregious to a Black person or for a white institution to do something egregious systematically to many Black people. Situations of coequal power—among coworkers or students or teachers—are difficult to see as examples of sexual harassment unless you have a notion of male power. I think we lie to women when we call it not power when a woman is come onto by a man who is not her employer, not her teacher. What do we labor under, what do we feel, when a man—any man—comes and hits on us? I think we require women to feel fine about turning down male-initiated sex so long as the man doesn't have some *other* form of power over us. Whenever—every and any time—a woman feels conflicted and wonders what's wrong with her that she can't decline although she has no inclination, and she feels open to male accusations, whether they come from women or men, of "why didn't you just tell him to buzz off?" we have sold her out, not named her experience. We are taught that we exist for men. We should be flattered or at least act as if we are—be careful about a man's ego because you never know what he can do to you. To flat out say to him, "You?" or "I don't want to" is not *in* most women's sex-role learning. To say it is, is bravado. And that's because he's a man, not just because you never know what he can do to you because he's your boss (that's two things—he's a man and he's the boss) or your teacher or in some other hierarchy. It seems to me that we haven't talked very much about gender *as* a hierarchy, as a division of power, in the way that's expressed and acted out, primarily I think sexually. And therefore we haven't expanded the definition according to women's experience of sexuality, including our own sexual intimidation, of what things are sexual in this world. So men have also defined what can be called sexual about us. They say, "I was just trying to be affectionate, flirtatious and friendly," and we were just all felt up. We criticize the idea that rape comes down to her word against his—but it really *is* her perspective against his perspective, and the law has been written from his perspective. If he didn't mean it to be sexual, it's not sexual. If he didn't see it as forced, it wasn't forced. Which is to say, only male sexual violations, that is, only male ideas of what sexually violates us as women, are illegal. We buy into this when we say our sexual violations are abuses of power, not sex.

Just as rape is supposed to have nothing against intercourse, just as sexual harassment is supposed to have nothing against normal sexual initiation (men initiate, women consent—that's mutual?), the idea that pornography is violence against women, not sex, seems to distinguish artistic creation on the one hand from what is degrading to women on the other. It is candid and true but not enough to say of pornography, as Justice Stewart said, "I know it when I see it." *He* knows what he thinks it is when he sees it—but is that what *I* know? Is that the same "it"? Is he going to know what I know when I see it? I think pretty much not, given what's on the newsstand, given what is not considered hardcore pornography. Sometimes I think what is obscene is what does *not* turn on the Supreme Court—or what revolts them more. Which is uncommon, since revulsion is eroticized.

We have to admit that pornography turns men on; it is therefore erotic. It is a lie to say that pornography is not erotic. When we say it is violence, not sex, we are saying, there is this degrading to women, over here, and this erotic, over there, without saying to whom. It is overwhelmingly disproportionately men to whom pornography is erotic. It is women, on the whole, to whom it is violent, among other things. And this is not just a matter of perspective, but a matter of reality.

Pornography turns primarily men on. Certainly they are getting something out of it. They pay incredible amounts of money for it; it's one of the largest industries in the country. If women got as much out of it as men do, we would buy it instead of cosmetics. It's a massive industry, cosmetics. We are poor but we have *some* money; we are some market. We spend our money to set ourselves up as the objects that emulate those images that are sold as erotic to men. What pornography says about us is that we enjoy degradation, that we are sexually turned on by being degraded. For me that obliterates the line, as a line at all, between pornography on one hand and erotica on the other, if what turns men on, what men find beautiful, is what degrades women. It is pervasively present in art, also, and advertising. But it is definitely present in eroticism, if that is what it is. It makes me think that women's sexuality as such is a stigma. We also sometimes have an experience of sexuality authentic somehow in all this. We are not allowed to have it; we are not allowed to talk about it; we are not allowed to speak of it or image it as from our own point of view. And, to the extent we try to assert that we are beings equal with men, we have to be either asexual or virgins.

To worry about cooptation is to realize that lies make bad politics. It is ironic that cooptation often results from an attempt to be "credible," to be strategically smart, to be "effective" on existing terms. Sometimes you become what you're fighting. Thinking about issues of sexual violation as issues of violence not sex could, if pursued legally, lead to opposing sexual harassment and pornography through morals legislation and obscenity laws. It is actually interesting that this theoretical stance has been widely embraced but these legal strategies have not been. Perhaps women realize that these legal approaches would not address the subordination of women to men, specifically and substantively. These approaches are legally as abstract as the "violence not sex" critique is politically abstract. They are both not enough and too much of the wrong thing. They deflect us from criticizing everyday behavior that is pervasive and normal and concrete and fuses sexuality with gender in violation and is not amenable to existing legal approaches. I think we need to think more radically in our legal work here.

Battering is called violence, rather than something sex-specific: this is done to women. I also think it is sexually done to women. Not only in where it is done—over half of the incidents are in the bedroom. Or the surrounding events—precipitating sexual jealousy. But when violence against women is eroticized as it is in this culture, it is very difficult to say that there is a major distinction in the level of sex involved between being assaulted by a penis and being assaulted by a fist, especially when the perpetrator is a man. If women as gender female are defined as sexual beings, and violence is eroticized, then men violating women has a sexual component. I think men rape women because they get off on it in a way that fuses dominance with sexuality. . . . I think that when men sexually harass women it expresses male control over sexual access to us. It doesn't mean they all want to fuck us, they just want to hurt us, dominate us, and control us, and that *is* fucking us. They want to be able to have that and to be able to say when they can have it, to *know* that. That is in itself erotic. The idea that opposing battering is about saving the family is, similarly, abstracted, gender-neutral. There are gender-neutral formulations of all these issues: law and order as opposed to derepression, Victorian morality as opposed to permissiveness, obscenity as opposed to art and freedom of expression. Gender-neutral, objective formulations like these avoid asking *whose* expression, from whose point of view? Whose law and whose order? It's not just a question of who is free to express ourselves; it's not just that there is almost no, if any, self-respecting women's eroticism. The fact is that what we do see, what we are allowed to experience, even in our own suffering, even in what we are allowed to complain about, is overwhelmingly constructed from the male point of view. Laws against sexual violation express what men see and do when they engage in sex with women; laws against obscenity center on the display of women's bodies in ways that men are turned on by viewing. To me, it not only makes us cooptable to define such abuses in gender-neutral terms like violence; when we fail to assert that we are fighting for the affirmative definition and control of our own sexuality, of our own lives as women, and that these experiences violate *that*, we have already been bought.

Radical feminism is not only critical of men's violence and sexuality, it turns male-dominated culture on its head. It takes all the characteristics that are valued by men in Western societies—objectivity, distance, control, coolness, aggressiveness, and competitiveness—and blames them for wars, poverty, rape, battering, child abuse, and incest. It praises what women do—feed and nurture, cooperate and reciprocate, and attend to bodies, minds, and psyches. The important values, radical feminism argues, are intimacy, persuasion, warmth, caring, and sharing—the characteristics that women develop in their hands-on, everyday experiences with their own and their children's bodies and with the work of daily living. Men could develop these characteristics, too, if they "mothered," but they are much more prevalent in women.

These arguments for the enormous value of mothering support the radical feminist perspective that teenage pregnancy and single parenting should not be automatically condemned. Pregnancy and childbirth are emotional as well as physical experiences. All mothers and children are equally valuable and need the support and services of governments and health care systems in addition to that of their families and communities.

The political implications of "maternal thinking" are laid out in the following excerpt by a writer on motherhood, peace, and feminism.

Maternal Thinking

Sara Ruddick

. . . Maternal thinking is only one aspect of "womanly" thinking. In articulating and respecting the maternal, I do not underwrite the still current, false, and pernicious identification of womanhood with biological or adoptive mothering of particular children in families. For me, "maternal" is a social category. Although maternal thinking arises out of actual child-caring practices, biological parenting is neither necessary nor sufficient. Many women and some men express maternal thinking in various kinds of working and caring with others. And some biological mothers, especially in misogynistic societies, take a fearful, defensive distance from their own mothering and the maternal lives of any women.

Maternal thought does, I believe, exist for all women in a radically different way than for men. It is because we are *daughters,* nurtured and trained by women, that we early receive maternal love with special attention to its implications for our bodies, our passions, and our ambitions. We are alert to the values and costs of maternal practices whether we are determined to engage in them or avoid them.

It is now argued that the most revolutionary change we can make in the institution of motherhood is to include men equally in every aspect of childcare. When men and women live together with children, it seems not only fair but deeply moral that they share in every aspect of childcare. To prevent or excuse men from maternal practice is to encourage them to separate public action from private affection, the privilege of parenthood from its cares. Moreover, even when men are absent from the nursery, their dominance in every other public and private room shapes a child's earliest conceptions of power. To familiarize children with "natural" domination at their earliest age in a context of primitive love, assertion, and sexual passion is to prepare them to find equally "natural" and exhaustive the division between exploiter and exploited that pervades the larger world. Although daughter and son alike may internalize "natural" domination, neither typically can live with it easily. Identifying with and imitating exploiters, we are overcome with self-hate; aligning ourselves with the exploited, we are fearful and manipulative. Again and again, family power dramas are repeated in psychic, interpersonal, and professional dramas, while they are institutionalized in economic, political, and international life. Radically recasting the power-gender roles in those dramas just might revolutionize social conscience.

Assimilating men into childcare both inside and outside the home would also be conducive to serious social reform. Responsible, equal childcaring would require men to relinquish power and their own favorable position in the division between intellectual/professional and service labor as that division expresses itself domestically. Loss of preferred status at home might make socially privileged men more suspicious of unnecessary divisions of labor and damaging hierarchies in the public world. Moreover, if men were emotionally and practically committed to childcare, they would reform the work world in parents' interests. Once no one "else" was minding the child, good day-care centers with flexible hours would be established to which parents could trust their children from infancy on. These day-care centers, like the workweek itself, would be managed flexibly in response to human needs as well as to the demands of productivity, with an eye to growth rather than measurable profit. Such moral reforms of economic life would probably begin with professions and managers servicing themselves. Even in nonsocialist countries, however, their benefits could be unpredictably extensive.

I would not argue that the assimilation of men into childcare is the primary social goal for mothers. Rather, we must work to bring a *transformed* maternal thought in the public realm, to make the preservation and growth of *all* children a work of public conscience and legislation. This will not be easy. Mothers are no less corrupted than anyone else by concerns of status and class. Often our misguided efforts on behalf of the success and purity of our children frighten them and everyone else around them. As we increase and enjoy our public effectiveness, we will have less reason to live vicariously through our children. We may then begin to learn to sustain a creative tension between our inevitable and fierce desire to foster our own children and the less compulsive desire that all children grow and flourish.

Nonetheless, it would be foolish to believe that mothers, just because they are mothers, can transcend class interest and implement principles of justice. All feminists must join in articulating a theory of justice shaped by and incorporating maternal thinking. Moreover, the generalization of attentive love to *all* children requires politics. The most enlightened thought is not enough.

Closer to home again, we must refashion our domestic life in the hope that the personal will in fact betoken the political. We must begin by resisting the temptation to construe "home" simplemindedly, as a matter of justice between mothers and fathers. Single parents, lesbian mothers, and coparenting women remind us that many ways to provide children with examples of caring do not incorporate sexual inequalities of power and privilege. Those of us who live with the fathers of our children will eagerly welcome shared parenthood—for overwhelming practical as well as ideological reasons. But in our eagerness, we must not forget that as long as a mother is not effective publicly and self-respecting privately, male presence can be harmful as well as beneficial. It does a woman no good to have the power of the Symbolic Father brought right into the nursery, often despite the deep, affectionate egalitarianism of an individual man. It takes a strong mother and father to resist temptations to domination and subordination for which they have been trained and are socially rewarded. And whatever the hard-won equality and mutual respect an individual couple may achieve, as long as a mother—even if she is no more parent than father—is derogated and subordinate outside the home, children will feel angry, confused, and "wildly unmothered."

Despite these reservations, I look forward to the day when men are willing and able to share equally and actively in transformed maternal practices. When that day comes, will we still identify some thought as maternal rather than merely parental? Might we echo the cry of some feminists—there shall be no more "women"—with our own—there shall be no more "mothers," only people engaging in childcare? To keep matters clear I would put the point differently. On that day there will be no more "fathers," no more people of either sex who have power over their children's lives and moral authority in their children's world, though they do not do the work of attentive love. There will be mothers of both sexes who live out a transformed maternal thought in communities that share parental care—practically, emotionally, economically, and socially. Such communities will have learned from their mothers how to value children's lives.

Reprinted from: Sara Ruddick, "Maternal Thinking," in *Rethinking the Family: Some Feminist Questions*, edited by Barrie Thorne, with Marilyn Yalom, pp. 89–91. Copyright © 1982 by The Institute for Research on Women & Gender, Stanford University. Reprinted by permission.

Radical feminism's view is that the presence of significant numbers of women can alter values and behavior because their ideas, their outlook, and their experiences are different from those of most men, almost to the point of giving women a different culture. *Eco-feminism* is a movement that applies maternal thinking and radical feminist ideas about the exploitation of women's bodies to protecting the environment and protesting against killing animals for fur and meat. The radical feminist praise of the qualities of women that derive from their nurturance and care of others, especially among those who speak of a woman's culture, has also led to feminist religions and ethics, and to the women's health care movement.

In *religion*, radical feminism argues that while more women clergy and gender-neutral liturgical language are very important in reforming religious practices, they do not make a religion less patriarchal unless there is also a place for women's prayers and rituals. So, at Passover, Jewish feminists hold all-women seders with specially written Haggadahs that tell of the Jews' exodus from Egypt and wanderings in the desert from a woman's point of view. They celebrate Miriam as well as Moses.

Feminist religious scholars have reinterpreted the history and text of the Old and New Testaments, showing the original influence of women spiritual leaders and their gradual exclusion as Christianity became institutionalized. Islamic feminists have found, in their reading of the Qur'an, that Mohammed intended women and men to be equal. Buddhism's many goddesses have been given a more important place in the pantheon by feminists.

As an alternative to teachings of organized religions, Catholic and Protestant feminist ethicists have developed an ethics that puts women's experiences at the center of moral choices. They work through an umbrella organization, called Woman-Church, that is composed of feminist groups engaged in reconstructing ethics and sexual morality. One of these groups, the Women's Alliance for Theology, Ethics, and Ritual (WATER), argues for the importance of considering situational contexts in moral judgments. Another group, Catholics for a Free Choice, says that the circumstances of a woman's life and that of her family should determine whether or not an abortion is justified.

Other radical feminists have discarded a traditional religious affiliation altogether and have formed wiccas, or witch's covens. Some feminist spiritual circles have derived their symbols and rituals from the earth and fertility goddesses of pre-Judeo-Christian and pre-Islamic religions. They say that the Virgin Mary is a cultural descendent of a fertility goddess, the Queen of the May, and that three pre-Islamic fertility goddesses were transformed into the daughters of Allah. The Teotihuacan Feathered Serpent of many Mexican cultures originally represented a goddess, and the introduction of Christianity by the Spaniards uprooted the native culture's Corn Mothers. In reviving women-centered religions, radical spiritual feminism is reclaiming women's sexuality, pregnancy and childbirth, menstruation, and menopause from men who have made them into sins or illnesses.

In *medicine*, the women's health care movement resisted medical practices dominated by men; at first, they did so outside of mainstream institutions, but then many of their recommended changes were incorporated into the mainstream. Many women entered medical school in the 1960s and 1970s in the United States and other countries where most of the physicians had been men, but they found it very difficult to change curricula or training. At that time, men's bodies were the norm in textbooks; women's bodies were a deviation because they menstruated and gave birth. Standard medical practice has treated normal pregnancies as illnesses and has used monitors and machines routinely in normal childbirth, distancing women from their own bodies. The new reproductive technologies for infertile couples detach conception from sexual intimacy: for example, in a petri dish, sperm produced by masturbation are mixed with ova that are harvested surgically.

In the 1970s in the United States, the women's health movement tried to take the control of women's bodies out of the hands of the medical system because the care women patients were getting from men doctors took few of their overall needs into consideration and allowed them very little control over their treatment. The solution was women-run clinics for women patients. Nurses and other health care workers taught gynecological self-examination, took a whole-person approach to diagnosis and treatment, and dispensed alternative medicines. The women's health movement did not consider women physicians to be much better than men physicians, since they had been trained in the same medical schools and hospitals. The activists in the women's health movement thought that by educating women patients to be more assertive and knowledgeable health consumers, they would put pressure on the medical system to modify the way men and women physicians are taught to practice.

The women's health movement has encouraged the training and employment of midwives and the experience of family-oriented childbirth at home and in birthing centers separated from hospitals. It has been critical of the new reproductive technologies, breast implants, and cosmetic surgery as violations of women's bodily integrity. The consumer movement in medicine has taken over most of the women's health movement's demands that medicine become more holistic and patient-oriented. Adapting the radical feminist critique and working within mainstream medicine, women physicians in the United States have, in the last few years, promoted research and held conferences on women's medical needs and have published a medical journal devoted to research on women's health. They have pushed for women to be part of all clinical trials for new drugs and have collected statistics on the likelihood of women to contract "men's" illnesses, such AIDS and heart disease. Female bodies are no longer seen as a deviation from a male norm; rather, the definition of "normal" has been altered.

Critique. Radical feminism is a direct and open confrontation with the gendered social order. Its condemnation of Western society's encouragement of men's violence and aggressive sexuality has led to a critique of the unequal power in heterosexual relationships. It defends the value of mothering over paid work. Thus, it produces a schism among feminists, offending many of those who are in heterosexual relationships, who do not want children, or who are ambitious for careers. The contrast of women's emotional and nurturing capabilities with men's intrusive sexuality and aggressiveness in cultural feminism has been seen as *essentialist*—rooted in deep-seated and seemingly intractable differences between two global categories of people.

This concentration on pervasive gender characteristics and oppression has led to accusations that radical feminism neglects racial, ethnic, religious, and social class differences among men and among women, and that it downplays other sources of oppression. However, radical feminism has joined with marxist, socialist, and development feminisms in political activism to improve the lives of poor and working class women of disadvantaged racial ethnic groups in industrial and nonindustrial countries.

Another divisive issue has been radical feminism's views on sexuality and pornography's harmfulness. Some feminists do not think pornography is that harmful to women, unlike radical feminists, who are in the forefront of the fights against sexual exploitation, harassment, rape, and battering. Radical feminism's stance against sadomasochism and other forms of "kinky" sex at the 1981 Barnard College conference, "The Scholar and the Feminist IX: Toward a Politics of Sexuality," opened a feminist "sex war" that has not died down to this day.

Yet it was radical feminism's extremism ("radical" means down to the roots) and fury at the throwaway use of women's bodies, sexuality, and emotions that made men and women realize how deeply misogynist our supposedly enlightened social world is. Radical feminism deserves much credit for bringing rape, sexual abuse of children, battering, and sexual harassment to public attention. Those who try to raise the value of women by praising motherhood have been criticized by feminists who feel this strategy invokes traditional rationales for keeping women out of the public arena. But it does what some radical feminists want—to put women on the social map as different from men but worth just as much, if not more.

Summary

It may seem as if some radical feminists' slogan could be, "Women are not just as good as men, they are *better.*" (Others strongly repudiate such views.) If men are so violent and sexually aggressive, and women are so nurturant and emotionally sensitive, what the world needs is for women, not men, to run things. As leaders, women would be less hierarchical and authoritarian, more cooperative and consensual. They would respect the environment. Ethically, they would look out for others' needs, and spiritually, they would form loving, caring communities that included men.

Despite this utopian vision, radical feminism's practical actions focus on setting up rape crisis centers and battered women's shelters, teaching women karate and other forms of self-defense, developing guidelines against sexual harassment, and educating people about date rape. Radical feminist politics mounts campaigns against prostitution, pornography, and other forms of sex work, as well as against high-tech reproductive technologies, breast implants, cosmetic surgery, and other types of demeaning objectification of women's bodies.

Radical feminism was the theoretical rationale for women's studies programs in colleges and universities. It is not enough to add women to the curriculum as another social group to be studied; women's ways of thinking have to be brought to the forefront. Women's bodies, sexuality, and emotional relationships are different from men's, and so is women's literature, art, music, and crafts. If most of what is taught in schools is "men's studies," then what is needed is a separate focus on women's history, knowledge, and culture.

The same argument—that it is not enough to "add women and stir" but that women's experiences produce a radical rethinking—occurs in feminist ethics, religions, and medicine. Women's ethics are based on responsibility to others, not individual rights; women's religious rituals focus on their life cycles, not men's; and women's health care tends to the social as well as physical problems of girls and women.

Organizationally, radical feminists form non-hierarchical, supportive, woman-only spaces where women can think and act and create free of constant sexist put-downs, sexual harassment, and the threat of rape and violence. The heady possibilities of creating woman-oriented health care facilities, safe residences for battered women, counseling and legal services for survivors of rape, a woman's culture, and a woman's religion and ethics forge the bonds of sisterhood. Politically, their primary mission is fighting for women and against men's social supremacy.

Radical feminism, by refusing to go along with conventional assumptions, directly confronts the deep-seated denigration and control of women in the gendered social order. It pushes feminism into direct conflict with those in power. The battle cry is no longer "Women deserve equal rights," but "Sisterhood is powerful."

Suggested Readings in Radical Feminism

Adams, Carol J., and Josephine Donovan (eds.). 1995. *Animals and Women: Feminist Theoretical Explorations*. Durham, NC: Duke University Press.

Bart, Pauline B., and Eileen Geil Moran (eds.). 1993. *Violence Against Women: The Bloody Footprints.* Newbury Park, CA: Sage.

Daly, Mary. 1978. *Gyn/Ecology: The Metaethics of Radical Feminism.* Boston: Beacon Press.

Gilligan, Carol. 1982. *In a Different Voice.* Cambridge, MA: Harvard University Press.

Gimbutas, Marija. 1989. *The Language of the Goddess.* San Francisco: Harper and Row.

Jayakar, Pupul. 1990. *The Earth Mother: Legends, Ritual Arts, and Goddesses of India.* San Francisco: Harper & Row.

Knight, Chris. 1991. *Blood Relations: Menstruation and the Origins of Culture.* New Haven, CT: Yale University Press.

MacKinnon, Catharine A. 1989. *Toward a Feminist Theory of the State.* Cambridge, MA: Harvard University Press.

Merchant, Carolyn. [1980] 1989. *The Death of Nature: Women, Ecology, and the Scientific Revolution.* New York: Harper & Row.

Morgan, Robin (ed.). 1970. *Sisterhood Is Powerful.* New York: Vintage.

O'Brien, Mary. 1981. *The Politics of Reproduction.* New York: Routledge & Kegan Paul.

Rothman, Barbara Katz. 1989. *Recreating Motherhood: Ideology and Technology in a Patriarchal Society.* New York: Norton.

Ruether, Rosemary Radford. 1983. *Sexism and God-talk: Toward a Feminist Theology.* Boston: Beacon Press.

Ruether, Rosemary Radford, and Eleanor McLaughlin (eds.). 1979. *Women of Spirit: Female Leadership in the Jewish and Christian Traditions.* New York: Simon and Schuster.

Ruzek, Sheryl Burt. 1978. *The Women's Health Movement: Feminist Alternatives to Medical Control.* New York: Praeger.

Sabbah, Fatna A. 1984. *Woman in the Muslim Unconscious.* (Trans. by Mary Jo Lakeland). New York: Pergamon.

Chapter Five

Lesbian Feminism

Sources of Gender Inequality

- Oppressive heterosexuality
- Men's domination of women's social spaces

Remedies

- Empowering women-identified women
- Women-only workplaces, cultural events, and political organizations
- Lesbian sexual relationships

Contributions

- Critical analysis of heterosexual romantic love and sexual relationships
- Exploration of women's sexuality
- Expansion of lesbianism to include community and culture
- Dual battles for women's rights and for homosexual rights

L esbian feminism takes the radical feminist pessimistic view of men to its logical conclusion. If heterosexual relationships are intrinsically exploitative because of men's social, physical, and sexual power over women, why bother with men at all? Women are more loving, nurturant, sharing, and understanding. Men like having women friends to talk about their problems with, but women can only unburden to other women. "Why not go all the way?" asks lesbian feminism. Stop sleeping with the "enemy," and turn to other women for sexual love as well as for intellectual companionship and emotional support.

Lesbianism, like male homosexuality, had always been underground in the United States and other countries, but fired by the social protest movements of the 1960s, both became increasingly visible and acceptable as alternative ways to have intimate relationships. Up to the 1960s, many women professionals and activists, most of whom did not identify themselves as lesbians, were nonetheless able to break the mold of conventional women's roles because of their deeply emotional, supportive friendships with other women, which may or may not have been sexual.

Despite popular opinion, most feminists are not lesbians, and many lesbians are not feminists. There is a continuum of relationships, from life-long friendships among women who identify themselves as heterosexuals and whose sexual partners are men, to women-identified women who are politically active in causes benefitting women and whose sexuality is varied, to women who identify themselves as lesbians and whose sexual and emotional partners are exclusively women.

In the following excerpt, Lillian Faderman, who has written two histories of lesbianism, discusses the changing meaning of women's emotional involvement with other women.

Romantic Friendship and Lesbian Love

Lillian Faderman

Passionate romantic friendship between women was a widely recognized, tolerated social institution before our century. Women were, in fact, expected to seek out kindred spirits and form strong bonds. It was socially acknowledged that while a woman could not trust men outside her framily, she could look to another female for emotional sustenance and not fear betrayal. Had a woman of an earlier era *not* behaved with her intimate friend . . . [in an emotional manner], she would have been thought strangely cold. But her relationship to another female went beyond such affectionate exchanges. It was not unusual for a woman to seek in her romantic friendship the center of her life, quite apart from the demands of marriage and family if not in lieu of them. When women's role in society began to change, however—when what women did needed to be taken more seriously because they were achieving some of the powers that would make them adult persons—society's view of romantic friendship changed.

Love between women—relationships which were *emotionally* in no way different from the romantic friendships of earlier eras—became evil or morbid. It was not simply that men now saw the female sexual drive more realistically. Many of the relationships that they condemned had little to do with sexual expression. It was rather that love between women, coupled with their emerging freedom, might conceivably bring about the overthrow of heterosexuality—which has meant not only sex between men and women but patriarchal culture, male dominance, and female subservience. Learning their society's view of love between women, females were compelled to supress natural emotion; they were taught to see women only as rivals and men as their only possible love objects, or they were compelled to view themselves as "lesbian," which meant "twisted" either morally or emotionally. What was lovely and nurturing in love between women, what women of other centuries clearly understood, became one of the best-guarded secrets of the patriarchy.

In the sophisticated twentieth century women who chose to love women could no longer see themselves as romantic friends, unless they enveloped themselves in a phenomenal amount of naiveté and were oblivious to modern psychology, literature, and dirty jokes. If they persisted in same-sex love past adolescence, they would at least have to take into account what society thought of lesbians, and they would have to decide to what extent they would internalize those social views. If they were unusually strong or had a strong support group, they might escape regarding themselves as sick sinners. For many of them, without models to show that love between women was not intrinsically wrong or unhealthy, the experts' pronouncements about lesbianism worked as a self-fulfilling prophecy. They became as confused and tormented as they were supposed to be. But it was only during this brief era in history that tragedy and sickness were so strongly attributed to (and probably for that reason so frequently found in) love between women.

This changed with the rise of the second wave of feminism. Having made a general challenge to patriarchal culture, many feminists in the last decade began to challenge its taboos on love between women too. They saw it as their job to divest themselves of all the prejudices that had been inculcated in them by their male-dominated society, to reexamine everything regarding women, and finally to reclaim the meaning of love between women. Having learned to question both the social order which made women the second sex and the meaning behind the taboos on love between women, they determined to live their lives through new definitions they would create. They called themselves women-identified-women, or they consciously attempted to lift the stigma from the term "lesbian" and called themselves lesbian-feminists, by which they meant that they would put women first in their lives because men had proven, if not on a personal then on a cultural scale, that they were not to be trusted. Lesbian-feminists see men and women as being at odds in their whole approach to the world: men, as a rule, are authoritarian, violent, cold, and women are the opposite. Like romantic friends before them, lesbian-feminists choose women, kindred spirits, for their love objects. Unlike most romantic friends, however, they understand through feminist doctrine the sociopolitical meaning of their choice.

Lesbian-feminists differ from romantic friends in a number of ways. Most significantly, the earlier women generally had no hope of actually spending their lives together despite often reiterated fantasies that they might; but also romantic friends did not have an articulated doctrine which would help them explain why they could feel closer to women than to men. And the primary difference which affected their relationship to the world is that romantic friends, unlike lesbian-feminists, seldom had reason to believe that society saw them as outlaws—even when they eloped together. . . . Lesbian-feminists understand, even when they are comfortable within a large support group, that the world outside views them as criminal and reduces their love to a pejorative term. Whatever anger they began with as feminists is multiplied innumerable times as lesbian-feminists as soon as they experience, either in reality or by observation, society's hostility to what is both logical and beautiful to them. Even if they do not suffer personally—if they do not lose their children in court or if they are not fired from their jobs or turned out by their families because of their political-sexual commitments—lesbian-feminists are furious, knowing that such possibilities exist and that many women do suffer for choosing to love other women. Romantic friends never learned to be angry through their love.

There is a good deal on which lesbian-feminists disagree, such as issues concerning class, whether or not to form monogamous relationships, the virtues of communal living, whether separatism is necessary in order to live as a lesbian-feminist, the nature of social action that is efficacious, etc. But they all agree that men have waged constant battle against women, committed atrocities or at best injustices against them, reduced them to grown-up children, and that a feminist ought not to sleep in the enemy camp. They all agree that being a lesbian is, whether consciously or unconsciously perceived, a political act, a refusal to fulfill the male image of womanhood or to bow to male supremacy. Perhaps for romantic friends of other eras their relationship was also a political act, although much more covert: With each other they could escape from many of the externally imposed demands of femininity that were especially stringent throughout much of the eighteenth and nineteenth centuries. They could view themselves as human beings and prime rather than as the second sex. But they did not hope that through their relationship they might change the social structure. Lesbian-feminists do.

They see their lesbian-feminism not just as a personal choice regarding life-style, even though it is certainly a most personal choice. But it is also a political choice which challenges sexism and heterosexism. It is a choice which has been made often in the context of the feminist movement and with an awareness of the ideology behind it. It has seemed the only possible choice for many women who believe that the personal is political, that to reject male supremacy in the abstract but to enter into a heterosexual relationship in which the female is usually subservient makes no sense. Contemporary lesbianism, on the other hand, makes a great deal of sense. It is a combination of the natural love between women, so encouraged in the days of romantic friendships, with the twentieth-century women's freedom that feminism has made possible.

While romantic friends had considerable latitude in their show of physical affection toward each other, it is probable that, in an era when women were not supposed to be sexual, the sexual possibilities of their relationship were seldom entertained. Contemporary women can have no such innocence. But the sexual aspect of their lesbian-feminist relationships generally have less significance than the emotional sustenance and the freedom they have to define themselves. While many lesbian-feminist relationships can and do continue long after the sexual component has worn off, they cannot continue without emotional sustenance and freedom of self-definition. Romantic friends of other eras would probably have felt entirely comfortable in many lesbian-feminist relationships had the contemporary label and stigma been removed.

But many women today continue to be frightened by love between women because the pejorative connotation of the contemporary label and stigma are still very real for them. Such fear is bound to vanish in the future as people continue to reject strict orthodoxy in sexual relationships: Women will be less and less scared off by the idea of same-sex love without examining what it entails beyond "sexual abnormality." The notion of lesbianism will be neutralized. As females are raised to be more independent, they will not assume that heterosexual marriage is necessary for survival and fulfillment; nor will they accept male definitions of womanhood or non-womanhood. They will have no need to repress natural feelings of affection toward other women. Love between women will become as common as romantic friendship was in other eras. The twentieth-century combination of romantic friendship and female independence will continue to yield lesbian-feminism.

In an ideal world lesbian-feminism, which militantly excludes relationships with men, would not exist. And, of course, the romantic friendships such as women were permitted to conduct in other centuries—in which they might be almost everything to each other but in which a male protector was generally needed in order for them to survive—would not exist either. Instead, in a utopia men would not claim supremacy either in social or personal relationships, and women would not feel that they must give up a part of themselves in order to relate to men. Women with ambition and strength and a sense of themselves would have no reason to see men as the enemy out to conquer and subdue them. Nor would there be any attempt to indoctrinate the female with the notion that to be normal she must transfer the early love she felt for her mother first to her father and then to a father substitute—a man who is more than she is in all ways: older, taller, better educated, smarter, stronger. Women as well as men would not select their love objects on the basis of sexual politics, in surrender or in reaction to an arbitrary heterosexual ideology. They would choose to love another only in reference to the individual needs of their own personalities, which ideally had been allowed to develop untrammelled and free of sex-role stereotyping. Potential or actual bisexuality, which is today looked on by lesbian-feminists as a political betrayal and by heterosexuals as an instability, would be normal, both emotionally and statistically.

But until men stop giving women cause to see them as the enemy and until there ceases to be coercion to step into prescribed roles without reference to individual needs and desires, lesbian-feminists will continue to view their choice as the only logical one possible for a woman who desires to be her own adult person.

As theory and in politics, lesbian feminism transforms love between women into an identity, a community, and a culture. Lesbian feminism praises women's sexuality and bodies, mother–daughter love, and the culture of women, thus expanding sexual and emotional relationships between women into a wholly engaged life. Politically, lesbian feminists fight on two fronts—for all women's betterment and for the civil rights and social worth of lesbians.

Whether lesbians identify and act politically mostly as homosexuals or mostly as women varies. In Germany today, there are three self-identified political categories—women, feminists, and lesbians. In the United States, lesbians first identified with homosexual men in their resistance to sexual discrimination, but after experiencing the same gender discrimination as women in the civil rights and draft-resistance movements, they turned to feminist organizations. There, unhappily, they experienced hostility to their sexuality from heterosexual women. Subsequently, some lesbian feminists developed an oppositional, woman-identified, separatist movement. But many lesbian activist groups welcome heterosexual women in their work for women's issues. Other lesbians have joined with gay men in their battle with the AIDS epidemic.

Lesbians are not monolithic. In the 1950s, lesbians playing the "fem" role were extremely feminine in their dress, demeanor, and expressions of sexuality, while "butches" were cool, masculine-looking, and assertive. There were also butch-fem role exchangers ("roll overs" or "kikis") who played both parts. Some lesbian women have biological children and raise them with a lesbian partner. Others have been critical of sexual monogamy, with or without children, as imitative of the institution of heterosexual marriage. These lesbians prefer alternative household arrangements of several partners, which may include gay men.

Lesbian feminism's defining stance on sexuality is that heterosexuality is oppressive and therefore women are better off having sexual relationships with women. But there are debates within lesbian feminism over the origin of women's sexual attraction to women—is it inborn and life-long or can it develop at any time, perhaps beginning with an intense work or political involvement? Another split in lesbian feminism is over sadomasochistic sexual relationships between women, which seem to violate the egalitarian and non-violent ethos of both feminism and lesbianism.

Bisexuality challenges lesbian feminism behaviorally and politically. Women bisexuals who have sexual relations with both women and men, sometimes simultaneously and sometimes serially, disturb the clear gender and sexual divisions that are the basis for woman-identification and lesbian separatism. Bisexuality may not undercut the identification with women as an oppressed social group, but it undermines the lesbian separatist solution. Paula Rust's sociological study of bisexuality and lesbianism explores the dilemmas for lesbian feminism that are posed by the possibility of a bisexual feminist political movement.

BISEXUAL POLITICS

Paula C. Rust

Many of the arguments that bisexuals are using to politicize bisexuality are very similar to arguments that lesbians used in the 1970s to politicize lesbianism. But there are also some important differences between the two movements, because the political arena in which bisexuals are struggling for recognition is substantially different from the one lesbians faced two decades ago. To a large extent, therefore, the bisexual movement is another revolution on the same political wheel, but perhaps the bisexual movement is also a revolution, period. To understand both possibilities, we have to look at the similarities and the differences between the lesbian movement of the early 1970s and the bisexual movement of the early 1990s.

The bisexual movement's roots in the lesbian/gay movement are analogous to the lesbian movement's roots in the feminist and gay movements. Contemporary bisexual activists concentrate much of their energy on building a home within the lesbian/gay movement by arguing that "bi liberation is gay liberation" and demanding that lesbian/gay organizations and events nominally and actually include bisexuals. Similarly, early lesbian feminists initially struggled to find a home within the feminist and gay movements. Like early lesbian feminists who argued that lesbians had been in the feminist movement all along but remained hidden because of feminists' homophobia, bisexuals argue that bisexuals have been in the lesbian/gay movement all along but remained hidden because of biphobia.

Lesbian feminists eventually lost patience with the homophobia of feminists and the sexism of gay men, and established an independent lesbian feminist movement. Among bisexuals, the vision of an independent bisexual movement is a minority opinion; the separatist BiCentrist Alliance is considered outside the mainstream of bisexual political thought. But at the same time, despite most activists' insistence that bisexuals rightfully belong in the lesbian/gay movement, they are building the structure of a separate bisexual movement complete with a national bisexual network and international conferences. Moreover, ideology is beginning to follow suit; most of the bisexual women who participated in my study in 1986 saw their interests as flowing from their genders and their "gayness," not from their bisexuality, whereas the bisexual activists whose opinions appeared in bisexual publications of the late 1980s and early 1990s identified unique bisexual interests. Whether the LesBiGay model of political organizing will continue to dominate bisexual political strategy, or whether bisexual ideology will continue to develop in an independent direction to be followed eventually by a shift in political strategy as occurred in the lesbian movement, remains to be seen.

One strategy used by both lesbians and bisexuals to politicize themselves is to present their movements as challenges to established ways of thinking. Lesbian feminists argued that heterosexuality is a political institution that upholds patriarchy and that lesbianism, as an alternative to heterosexuality, is therefore political and feminist. Early lesbian feminists also argued that lesbianism is feminist because it challenges gender—specifically, the male definition of feminine gender that defines a "real woman" as a female who has sex with men. Contrary to the feeling of feminists at the time that lesbians were marginal constituents of the feminist movement and that the movement should focus on the needs of "women," not "lesbians," lesbians argued that they were the quintessential women and that the movement should not only address lesbians' needs but recognize lesbians as the true feminists. Thus, lesbianism was initially constructed as a challenge to gender. But once "woman" was reconstructed to include "lesbian," lesbians became part of the prevailing gender structure. In effect, lesbianism was co-opted into gender and ceased to be a challenge to it. Furthermore, the rise of cultural feminism reified rather than challenged gender, maximized rather than minimized the differences between women and men, and created a concept of lesbianism that was dependent on the preservation of gender.

Similarly, bisexual activists argue that categorical Western thinking is oppressive because it limits people's options, and that bisexuality is political because it challenges categorical thinking. Specifically, bisexuality is a challenge to dichotomous thinking about both gender and sexuality. Because bisexuality challenges these dichotomies, it undermines oppression based on them, i.e., sexism and heterosexism. Therefore, if lesbianism is political and feminist, bisexuality is political, feminist, and queer. If lesbianism undermines the heteropatriarchy, bisexuality undermines not only the heteropatriarchy but the fundamental structure of Western thought.

Given lesbians' initial challenge to gender, one might expect bisexuals' efforts to break down gender to be well received among lesbians. But because of the change in the relationship of lesbianism to gender that occurred with the reconstruction of womanhood and the rise of cultural lesbian feminism, bisexuals' contemporary challenge to gender is also a threat to lesbianism. Lesbianism is now part of the gender establishment that bisexuals seek to break down. Bisexuals' challenge to gender is no less than a challenge to the very existence of lesbianism, because of the dependence of lesbianism on gender for definition. Instead of being allies in the struggle against gender, because of the course taken by lesbian feminism in the two decades before the inception of the bisexual movement, lesbians and bisexuals have emerged with contrary political goals in reference to gender.

Bisexuality's challenge to dichotomous sexuality poses a threat to lesbianism that is even more direct. Lesbians contributed to the construction of dichotomous sexuality, primarily through their efforts to construct lesbians as an ethnic group. To become an ethnic group, lesbians had to distinguish themselves from non-lesbians and create the appearance of clear and fixed boundaries between themselves as the oppressed and heterosexuals as the oppressor. Lesbians are now part of the society that is based on dichotomous ways of thinking. If bisexuals are a threat to sexual dichotomy, they are a threat to lesbians.

This threat is multiple. At the very least, bisexuals are a material threat to lesbians because as the new category "bisexual" becomes available as an alternative to the homosexual/heterosexual dichotomy, some women who would otherwise have placed themselves in the lesbian category will place themselves in the new bisexual category. Lesbians will therefore lose numbers. However, the real threat is not to the size of the lesbian population, but to the ethnicity of lesbianism. By challenging and ultimately destroying the sexual dichotomy, bisexuals threaten to undermine the clarity of the distinction between lesbians and heterosexuals. If some people are bisexual—particularly if that bisexuality is conceptualized in hybrid terms—then the distinction between homosexuality and heterosexuality is not clear at all. If some people are both homosexual and heterosexual, then lesbians cannot be clearly distinguished from heterosexuals. If lesbians cannot be clearly distinguished from heterosexuals, then how can they claim to be oppressed by heterosexuals, and how can they struggle to win their liberation from heterosexuals? If the sexual dichotomy is destroyed, lesbians are deprived of their ethnicity, and of the strategies for liberation that flow from ethnicity.

If bisexuals were to construct themselves as an ethnic group, then the threat to lesbianism would be alleviated. The sexual dichotomy would be replaced by a sexual trichotomy, and the clarity of the category "lesbian" could be restored. But bisexuals show little indication that they will take this path, at least not in the near future. One might argue that the bisexual movement is simply too young to have yet constructed itself as an ethnic movement, but the lack of attention bisexuals are giving to the question of defining bisexuality stands in sharp contrast to the lively debates that occurred among lesbians on this issue in the early 1970s. The prevailing message in the bisexual press is that bisexuals should avoid establishing a single definition of bisexuality based on identifiable common characteristics, and little effort is being made to create bisexual ancestors or a bisexual heritage. Bisexuals are not constructing themselves as an ethnic group, precisely because they wish to remain a challenge to dichotomous gender and dichotomous sexuality. In so doing, they are not only refusing to place themselves into the ethnic political tradition; they are threatening to remove all of sexual identity politics from the realm of ethnic political discourse, thereby destroying other sexual minorities' abilities to utilize the language of ethnic politics to make their political claims.

Another strategy lesbian feminists used to politicize lesbianism was the desexualization of lesbianism. Because they were struggling to find a political voice in a period when sexuality was not recognized as political, to present themselves as political they had to distance themselves from sexuality. The rise of cultural feminism facilitated this effort by recalling the ideal of asexual womanly purity. But lesbians' efforts to politicize lesbianism contributed to the development of a sexual politics, and lesbians' efforts to desexualize lesbianism was one impetus for the rise of sex positivism. When bisexual activists appeared in the arena, sexuality was already politicized and sex positivism was in full swing. Because sex positivism is consistent with the bisexual emphasis on diversity, it was easily incorporated into the developing bisexual ideology, and because sexuality was politicized, this move was not antithetical to the process of bisexual politicization. Because of the historical period in which the bisexual movement has emerged, bisexuals can present themselves as both sexual and political; they can and do celebrate sexuality while simultaneously demanding recognition of their political voice.

Although they have largely escaped the desexualizing influence of lesbian feminism, bisexuals, especially bisexual women, cannot ignore the relationship that lesbian feminism constructed between lesbianism and feminism. . . . Lesbian feminists first constructed lesbianism as consistent with feminism, and then argued that lesbians are the best feminists because they are independent of men and have the vision and resources to create women's space. According to this analysis, bisexual women collaborate with the enemy (men) and are, in some senses, even more detrimental to the feminist movement than heterosexual women are. Contemporary bisexual activists, having claimed that bisexuality is feminist, have to reconstruct the relationship between feminism and sexuality to support their claim. Among the specific problems they face are how to build a mixed-gender movement that is feminist, and whether to welcome transgenderists to women's space within that movement. Building a feminist mixed-gender movement means challenging the argument that feminism depends on women's space and refuting the charge that by associating with men bisexuals are collaborating with the enemy. Welcoming transgenderists requires that bisexual women reject the reification of gender that took place with the growth of cultural feminism. Neither task will be easy, but their importance to bisexual women is evident in the number of authors who have addressed the task of constructing a feminist bisexuality.

Another difference between the lesbian and bisexual movements that is attributable to the different contexts in which they developed lies in their willingness to universalize their identities and interests. Many early lesbian feminists declared that "all women are lesbians." This claim served to present the lesbian movement as a movement for all women, and was based either on a concept of universal bisexuality, on arguments about the artificiality of culturally imposed heterosexuality, or on the redefinition of lesbianism as a form of feminist resistance. The concept of a universal bisexuality seems ready-made for a bisexual movement that might also want to emphasize its broad applicability and large constituency, but surprisingly, this idea has not been picked up enthusiastically by activists writing in the bisexual press. It was expressed by many of the bisexual women who took part in my study in 1986, but the fact that it does not appear consistently in the bisexual press suggests that the bisexual women in my study encountered the idea within lesbian feminism and found it personally gratifying. As such, it was evidence of the influence lesbian ideology had on them, not evidence of the beginnings of a bisexual ideology. Instead of proclaiming "everyone is bisexual," activists warn each other to respect the self-identities of those who choose not to identify as bisexual. The fact that bisexuals advocate respect for others' self-identities reflects the fact that the bisexual movement is developing in a context in which sexuality has already been politicized and lesbians and gay men have already constituted themselves as interest groups and invested heavily in their identities. . . .

This does not imply that lesbian feminists did not also consider self-identity important. They did, but for very different reasons than bisexuals. At the height of lesbian feminism, identity was considered a political statement, or a means toward an end. Women should, therefore, identify themselves as lesbians for political reasons regardless of what they thought they "really" were sexually. In contrast, bisexuals consider self-identity important because self-determination is important; bisexual identity is not an identity to be adopted for political reasons, but because that is how one wishes to define oneself for whatever reason, and others should respect that self-definition. This might be partially due to the early stage of the bisexual movement; after all, early lesbian feminists also advocated the right of women to sexual self-determination. As bisexual ideology develops and bisexuality acquires specific political meanings, it is quite possible that individuals will begin to adopt bisexual identity for political reasons. . . .

Finally, the role of race and ethnicity within the lesbian and bisexual movements differs, largely because of the different historical time periods in which the two movements developed. Lesbian feminism began, and remained, primarily a white movement. Lesbians who felt that the movement should pay attention to racial and ethnic issues shouldered the burden of calling other lesbians' attention to the problem and constructing elaborate arguments about the relationships among oppressions in order to convince them of the importance of the issue. Considerable debate occurred over the exact relationship among different oppressions; for example, do all oppressions arise from the same root, or is one oppression fundamental? If one is fundamental, is it classism, racism, or sexism? Contemporary bisexual activists not only inherit these arguments, but have come forth in a historical period in which the celebration of racial/ethnic diversity and efforts to eliminate racial/ethnic oppression need no justification. Therefore, they do not spend a great deal of energy asserting that the bisexual movement should be multicultural. From its inception, bisexuals declared the movement to be multicultural; the work that remains is the work of making sure that it is in fact multicultural.

In summary, bisexuals, like lesbians, are faced with the task of politicizing a sexual identity, but bisexuals live in a very different political world than early lesbian feminists did. Not only have politics in general changed in the intervening two decades, but the lesbian/gay movement itself has created an entirely new political tradition. As a result of the lesbian/gay movement, sexuality has been politicized, and lesbians and gays are established political interest groups. To establish their own political voice, bisexuals must insert themselves into an ongoing discourse of sexual identity politics. In a very real sense, the lesbian/gay movement created bisexuals as an oppressed group by creating a discourse in which lesbians/gays and heterosexuals, but not bisexuals, were defined into political existence. Thus, the lesbian/gay movement not only altered the political arena by creating a new political tradition; it also created the need for a bisexual movement.

To politicize bisexual identity, bisexuals are using some of the same arguments and strategies that lesbians used to politicize lesbian identity. Just as lesbians initially challenged traditional gender and recognized that the demise of gender would render their own sexual identities meaningless, bisexuals are presenting bisexuality as a challenge to dichotomous gender and dichotomous sexuality. In so doing, both movements challenge established ways of thinking and promise to contribute to the breakdown of oppression based on gender and sexuality. For this reason, both movements envision themselves as sexual liberation movements, and both consider themselves feminist movements.

But beyond these similarities, there are differences that reflect the different political contexts of the two movements. For example, to politicize lesbianism, lesbians had to desexualize it, whereas contemporary bisexuals can claim both their sexuality and their political voice because the sex-positive movement and the politicization of sexuality have made it possible to have both. Lesbians constructed a relationship between lesbianism and feminism that established lesbians as the best feminists and bisexuals as traitors; bisexuals must now reconstruct that relationship to support their claim that the bisexual movement is a feminist movement. Lesbian feminists initially valued sexual self-determination for women, but after developing a clear political ideology they began to see lesbian identity as an identity every woman can and should adopt. Contemporary bisexual activists advocate respect for individuals' sexual self-definitions, but they avoid the argument that all people can and should become bisexual-identified because they, unlike early lesbian feminists, face a political arena in which others already have political sexual self-identities that demand respect. Finally, lesbian feminists spent considerable energy discussing the relationships between sexism, heterosexism, racism, and classism to demonstrate the importance of taking race and class into account. Bisexuals take the importance of multiculturalism for granted, because lesbian feminism has already made the necessary connections and because society in general is more cognizant of the pervasive importance of race, class, ability, etc., and the need to actively struggle against all forms of oppression.

Because bisexuals are attempting to assert themselves in an ongoing political discourse in which lesbians have a considerable stake, bisexuals pose a challenge to lesbians. Lesbians have become invested in a gender-based definition of lesbianism. Bisexuals, by challenging both dichotomous gender and dichotomous sexuality, challenge the very existence of lesbianism. By refusing to construct themselves as an ethnic group, bisexuals undermine lesbian ethnicity and threaten the tenuous legitimacy all sexual identity-based minorities have gained in the realm of ethnic political discourse. Defined out of existence by lesbian feminism, bisexuals now threaten the existence of lesbianism and the future of the lesbian movement as we know it. . . .

Critique. Lesbian feminism began by claiming that all women can be considered lesbian in their emotional identification with women, even though they may be heterosexual in their sexual relationships. This gender identification was soon submerged by an insistence that lesbian sexual relationships are more feminist than heterosexual relationships, because intimacy with a man undercuts a woman's independence. But feminists who take up with women for political reasons in turn annoy lesbians who feel that sexual orientation is not something you can turn off and on.

A second unresolved argument is over the structure of lesbian relationships. The ideal type of lesbian relationship has been conventionalized as a sexually monogamous, emotionally satisfying bond between two loving women, weakening the critical edge of the lesbian boycott of the conventional family. Even if the structure of lesbian relationships resembles that of heterosexual pairs, lesbians argue that the quality of their relationships is entirely different. Free of male dominance, partners can be fully egalitarian and reciprocal in their behavior toward each other. Many lesbians, like many gay men, would like to have the legal benefits of marriage. They do not see why they, and not heterosexual feminists, have to give up the goal of legally recognized couple relationships to fight against the subordination of women in the traditional family.

Summary

As an offshoot of radical feminism, lesbian feminism pushes the critique of heterosexuality and conventional family life to its logical extreme. Theoretically, lesbian feminism argues that all heterosexual relationships, especially those that are romantic and sexual, are intrinsically coercive of women. Given men's dominant social position and tendency to oppress women in everyday interaction, it is better to have as little to do with them as possible. Women have to work with men and deal with them in many public arenas, but in their private lives and especially in sexual relationships, a woman is a far better partner.

Lesbian feminist separatists go further, and create cultural communities, social lives, and political organizations that are for women only.

Caring, nurturance, intimacy, and woman-to-woman love of all kinds are the ideals of these women's worlds. In recent years, however, the boundaries between lesbians and heterosexual feminists and between lesbians and gay men are giving way. Lesbians invite heterosexual women into their feminist political activities, and they work with gay men in political work. With the advent of men's feminism, lesbian feminism is less wary of even heterosexual men. In many political organizations today, neither gender nor sexual orientation are significant markers of who sides with whom.

Suggested Readings in Lesbian Feminism

Allen, Jeffner (ed.). 1990. *Lesbian Philosophies and Cultures*. Albany: State University of New York Press.

Faderman, Lillian. 1981. *Surpassing the Love of Men: Romantic Friendship and Love Between Women from the Renaissance to the Present*. New York: William Morrow.

——. 1991. *Odd Girls and Twilight Lovers: A History of Lesbian Life in Twentieth-Century America*. New York: Columbia University Press.

Frye, Marilyn. 1983. *The Politics of Reality: Essays in Feminist Theory*. Trumansburg, NY: The Crossing Press.

Hoagland, Sarah, and Julia Penelope (eds.). 1991. *For Lesbians Only: A Separatist Anthology*. London: Radical Feminist Lesbian Publishers.

Johnston, Jill. 1973. *Lesbian Nation: The Feminist Solution*. New York: Simon and Schuster.

Lorde, Audre. 1984. *Sister Outsider*. Trumansburg, NY: The Crossing Press.

Phelan, Shane. 1989. *Identity Politics: Lesbian Feminism and the Limits of Community*. Philadelphia: Temple University Press.

Rust, Paula C. 1995. *Bisexuality and the Challenge to Lesbian Politics: Sex, Loyalty, and Revolution*. New York: New York University Press.

Snitow, Ann, Christine Stansell, and Sharon Thompson (eds.). 1983. *Powers of Desire: The Politics of Sexuality*. New York: Monthly Review Press.

Vance, Carole S. (ed.). 1984. *Pleasure and Danger: Exploring Female Sexuality*. Boston: Routledge & Kegan Paul.

Wittig, Monique. 1992. *The Straight Mind and Other Essays*. Boston: Beacon Press.

Chapter Six

Psychoanalytic Feminism

Sources of Gender Inequality

- Gendered personality structures—ego-bound men and ego-permeable women
- Men's sublimated fear of women
- Cultural domination of men's phallic-oriented ideas and repressed emotions

Remedies

- Shared parenting, so men as well as women parent intensively
- Cultural productions that feature women's emotions, sexuality, and connectedness with the body

Contributions

- Analysis of the unconscious sources of masculinity and femininity
- Making evident the dominance of the *phallus* (symbol of masculine power) in Western culture
- Counteracting with literature written out of women's experiences with their bodies, sexuality, and emotions

In the 1970s, British, American, and French feminists began to reread and reinterpret Freud. Instead of Freud's primary focus on the personality development of boys, psychoanalytic feminism gives equal attention to the personality development of girls. It locates the origins of Freud's theories in the European patriarchal family structure of the early twentieth century and criticizes the extensive cultural and social effects of men's fear of castration, men's emotional repression, and their ambivalence toward women.

Psychoanalytic feminism claims that the source of men's domination of women is men's unconscious ambivalent need for women's emotionality and their simultaneous rejection of women as potential castrators. Women submit to men because of women's unconscious desires for emotional connectedness. These gendered personalities are the outcome of the *Oedipus complex*—the psychological separation from the mother as the child develops a sense of individual identity.

Because the woman is the primary parent, infants bond with her. According to Freudian theory, boys have to separate from their mothers and identify with their fathers in order to establish their masculinity. This identification causes them to develop strong ego boundaries and a capacity for the independent action, objectivity, and rational thinking so valued in Western culture. Women are a threat to their independence and masculine sexuality because they remind men of their dependence on their mothers. However, men need women for the emotional sustenance and intimacy they rarely give each other. Their ambivalence towards women comes out in heterosexual love-hate relationships.

Girls continue to identify with their mothers, and so they grow up with fluid ego boundaries that make them sensitive, empathic, and emotional. It is these qualities that make them potentially good mothers and keep them open to men's emotional needs. But because the men in their lives have developed personalities that are emotionally guarded, women want to have children to bond with. Thus, psychological gendering of children is continually reproduced. To develop nurturing capabilities in men, and to break the cycle of the reproduction of gendered personality structures, psychoanalytic feminism recommends shared parenting—after men are taught how to parent with emotional intimacy.

In an article published in 1976 in a special issue of *Social Problems*, "Feminist Perspectives: The Sociological Challenge," sociologist and psychoanalyst Nancy Chodorow laid out the processes and consequences of the Oedipus complex for women and men. It is a brief summary of the psychoanalytic theories presented in her influential book, *The Reproduction of Mothering*.

Oedipal Asymmetries and Heterosexual Knots

Nancy J. Chodorow

As a result of being parented by a woman, both sexes are looking for a return to this emotional and physical union. A man achieves this directly through the heterosexual bond which replicates for him emotionally the early mother-infant exclusivity which he seeks to recreate. He is supported in this endeavor by women, who, through their own development, have remained open to relational needs, have retained an ongoing inner affective life, and have learned to deny the limitations of masculine lovers for both psychological and practical reasons.

Men, generally, though, both look for and fear exclusivity. Throughout their development, they have tended to repress their affective relational needs and sense of connection, and to develop and be more comfortable with ties based more on categorical and abstract role expectations, particularly in relation to other males. Even when they participate in an intimate heterosexual relationship, it is likely to be with the ambivalence created by an intense relationship which one both wants and fears, demanding from women, then, what they are at the same time afraid of receiving. The relationship to the mother thus builds itself directly into contradictions in masculine heterosexual commitment.

As a result of being parented by a woman and growing up heterosexual, women have different and a more complex set of relational needs, in which exclusive relationship to a man is not enough. This is because women experience themselves as part of a relational triangle in which their father and men are emotionally secondary, or at most equal, in importance to their mother and women. Women, therefore, need primary relationships to women as well as to men. In addition, the relation to the man itself has difficulties. Idealization, growing out of a girl's relation to her father, involves denial of real feelings and to a certain extent an unreal relationship to men.

The contradictions in women's heterosexual relationships, though, do not inhere only in the outcome of early childhood relationships. As I have suggested, men themselves, because of their own development and socialization, grow up rejecting their own and others' needs for love, and, therefore, find it difficult and threatening to meet women's emotional needs. Thus, given the masculine personality which women's mothering produces, the emotional secondariness of men to women, and the social organization of gender and gender roles, a woman's relationship to a man is unlikely to provide satisfaction for the particular relational needs which women's mothering and the concomitant social organization of gender have produced in women.

The two structural principles of the family, then, are in contradiction with each other. The family reproduces itself in form: for the most part people marry, and marry heterosexually; for the most part, people form couples heterosexually. At the same time, it undercuts itself in content: as a result of men and women growing up in families where women mother, these heterosexual relations, married or not, are liable to be strained in the regularized ways I have described.

In an earlier period, father absence was less absolute, production centered in the home, and economic interdependence of the sexes meant that family life and marriage was not and did not have to be a uniquely or fundamentally emotional project. The heterosexual asymmetry which I have been discussing was only one aspect of the total marital enterprise, and, therefore, did not overwhelm it. Women in this earlier period could seek relationships to other women in their daily work and community. With the development of industrial capitalism, however—and the increasingly physically isolated, mobile, and neolocal nuclear family it has produced—other primary relationships are not easy to come by on a routine, daily, ongoing basis. At the same time, the public world of work, consumption, and leisure leaves people increasingly starved for affection, support, and a sense of unique self. The heterosexual relationship itself gains in emotional importance at the very moment when the heterosexual strains which mothering produces are themselves sharpened. In response to these emerging contradictions, divorce rates soar, people flock to multitudes of new therapies, politicians decry and sociologists document the end of the family. And there develops a new feminism.

In France, feminists took on the Freudian-oriented cultural critics Jacques Lacan and Jacques Derrida, who say that women cannot create culture because they lack a sense of difference (from the mother) and a phallus (identification with the powerful father). French psychoanalytic feminism focuses on the ways that cultural productions (novels, drama, art, opera, music, movies) reflect and represent the masculine unconscious, especially fear of castration. In French feminist psychoanalytic theory, a major part of patriarchal culture reflects the sublimation of men's suppressed infantile desire for the mother and fear of the loss of the phallus, the symbol of masculine difference from powerless women. Women's wish for a phallus and repressed sexual desire for their fathers is sublimated into wanting to give birth to a son; men's repressed sexual desire for their mothers and fear of the father's castration of them are sublimated into cultural creations.

Phallic cultural productions, according to psychoanalytic feminism, are full of men's aggression, competition between men, men's flight from women or domination of them. The underlying subtext is fear of castration—of becoming women. What women represent in phallic culture is the sexual desire and emotionality men must repress in order to become like their fathers—men who are self-controlled and controlling of others. No matter what role women play in cultural productions, the *male gaze* sees them as potentially engulfing mothers or as potentially castrating objects of desire. Carmen must be killed over and over again.

To resist and to counter this phallic centrality with woman-centeredness, French feminism calls for women to write from their biographical experiences and their bodies—about menstruation, pregnancy, childbirth, intimacy with their mothers and their friends, their sexual desires for women as well as for men. Women's cultural productions will be very different from men's. Carmen can love—and live to love again.

Rather than reassuring men of their masculinity by submitting to their symbolic sexual domination, Hélène Cixous, a well-known French feminist, says women must use their heads and their mouths for themselves. She transforms the image of the Medusa, the head whose look turns men to stone (a symbol of castration), into an icon of women's sexual strength. The Medusa's laughing mouth (women's sexuality) is liberating: "You have only to look at the Medusa straight on to see her. And she is not deadly. She is beautiful and she is laughing" (p. 885). In the following excerpt from an article originally published in France,

Cixous tells women how to resist their suppression through the appropriation of culture for themselves.

THE LAUGH OF THE MEDUSA

Hélène Cixous

I shall speak about women's writing: about *what it will do*. Woman must write her self: must write about women and bring women to writing, from which they have been driven away as violently as from their bodies—for the same reasons, by the same law, with the same fatal goal. Woman must put herself into the text—as into the world and into history—by her own movement.

The future must no longer be determined by the past. I do not deny that the effects of the past are still with us. But I refuse to strengthen them by repeating them, to confer upon them an irremovability the equivalent of destiny, to confuse the biological and the cultural. Anticipation is imperative.

Since these reflections are taking shape in an area just on the point of being discovered, they necessarily bear the mark of our time—a time during which the new breaks away from the old, and, more precisely, the (feminine) new from the old (*la nouvelle de l'ancien*). Thus, as there are no grounds for establishing a discourse, but rather an arid millennial ground to break, what I say has at least two sides and two aims: to break up, to destroy; and to foresee the unforeseeable, to project.

I write this as a woman, toward women. When I say "woman," I'm speaking of woman in her inevitable struggle against conventional man; and of a universal woman subject who must bring women to their senses and to their meaning in history. But first it must be said that in spite of the enormity of the repression that has kept them in the "dark"—that dark which people have been trying to make them accept as their attribute—there is, at this time, no general woman, no one typical woman. What they have *in common* I will say. But what strikes me is the infinite richness of their individual constitutions: you can't talk about *a* female sexuality, uniform, homogeneous, classifiable into codes—any more than you can talk about one unconscious resembling another.

Women's imagina[tion] is inexhaustible, like music, painting, writing: their stream of phantasms is incredible.

I have been amazed more than once by a description a woman gave me of a world all her own which she had been secretly haunting since early childhood. A world of searching, the elaboration of a knowledge, on the basis of a systematic experimentation with the bodily functions, a passionate and precise interrogation of her erotogeneity. This practice, extraordinarily rich and inventive, in particular as concerns masturbation, is prolonged or accompanied by a production of forms, a veritable aesthetic activity, each stage of rapture inscribing a resonant vision, a composition, something beautiful. Beauty will no longer be forbidden.

I wished that that woman would write and proclaim this unique empire so that other women, other unacknowledged sovereigns, might exclaim: I, too, overflow; my desires have invented new desires, my body knows unheard-of songs. Time and again I, too, have felt so full of luminous torrents that I could burst—burst with forms much more beautiful than those which are put up in frames and sold for a stinking fortune. And I, too, said nothing, showed nothing; I didn't open my mouth, I didn't repaint my half of the world. I was ashamed. I was afraid, and I swallowed my shame and my fear. I said to myself: You are mad! What's the meaning of these waves, these floods, these outbursts? Where is the ebullient, infinite woman who, immersed as she was in her naiveté, kept in the dark about herself, led into self-disdain by the great arm of parental-conjugal phallocentrism, hasn't been ashamed of her strength? Who, surprised and horrified by the fantastic tumult of her drives (for she was made to believe that a well-adjusted normal woman has a . . . divine composure), hasn't accused herself of being a monster? Who, feeling a funny desire stirring inside her (to sing, to write, to dare to speak, in short, to bring out something new), hasn't thought she was sick? Well, her shameful sickness is that she resists death, that she makes trouble.

And why don't you write? Write! Writing is for you, you are for you; your body is yours, take it. I know why you haven't written. (And why I didn't write before the age of twenty-seven.) Because writing is at once too high, too great for you, it's reserved for the great—that is, for "great men"; and it's "silly." Besides, you've written a little, but in secret. And it wasn't good, because it was in secret, and because you punished yourself for writing, because you didn't go all the way; or because you wrote, irresistibly, as when we would masturbate in secret, not to go further, but to attenuate the tension a bit, just enough to take the edge off. And then as soon as we come, we go and make ourselves feel guilty—so as to be forgiven; or to forget, to bury it until the next time.

Write, let no one hold you back, let nothing stop you: not man; not the imbecilic capitalist machinery, in which publishing houses are the crafty, obsequious relayers of imperatives handed down by an economy that works against us and off our backs; and not *yourself*. Smug-faced readers, managing editors, and big bosses don't like the true texts of women—female-sexed texts. That kind scares them.

I write woman: woman must write woman. And man, man. So only an oblique consideration will be found here of man; it's up to him to say where his masculinity and femininity are at: this will concern us once men have opened their eyes and seen themselves clearly.

Now women return from afar, from always: from "without," from the heath where witches are kept alive; from below, from beyond "culture"; from their childhood which men have been trying desperately to make them forget, condemning it to "eternal rest." The little girls and their "ill-mannered" bodies immured, well-preserved, intact unto themselves, in the mirror. Frigidified. But are they ever seething underneath! What an effort it takes—there's no end to it—for the sex cops to bar their threatening return. Such a display of forces on both sides that the struggle has for centuries been immobilized in the trembling equilibrium of a deadlock. . . .

Write your self. Your body must be heard. Only then will the immense resources of the unconscious spring forth. Our naphtha will spread, throughout the world, without dollars—black or gold—nonassessed values that will change the rules of the old game.

To write. An act which will not only "realize" the decensored relation of woman to her sexuality, to her womanly being, giving her access to her native strength; it will give her back her goods, her pleasures, her organs, her immense bodily territories which have been kept under seal; it will tear her away from the superegoized structure in which she has always occupied the place reserved for the guilty (guilty of everything, guilty at every turn: for having desires, for not having any; for being frigid, for being "too hot"; for not being both at once; for being too motherly and not enough; for having children and for not having any; for nursing and for not nursing . . .)—tear her away by means of this research, this job of analysis and illumination, this emancipation of the marvelous text of her self that she must urgently learn to speak. A woman without a body, dumb, blind, can't possibly be a good fighter.

She is reduced to being the servant of the militant male, his shadow. We must kill the false woman who is preventing the live one from breathing. Inscribe the breath of the whole woman. . . .

Critique. Psychoanalytic theories of gender and sexuality are based on the bourgeois Western nuclear family, in which the woman is the prime parent and the man is emotionally distant from his children. Feminist psychoanalytic theories are just as narrowly based in a family consisting of two heterosexual parents. There are few tests of Freudian theories of each gender's personality development on single-parent and other types of households. The involvement of fathers in parenting varies enormously in societies throughout the world. Furthermore, it is not only heterosexual women who want the emotional attachment of mothering. Many lesbians who have deep and intense relationships with women also want children.

Psychoanalytic feminism's theory of culture is also too generalized— it assumes that all men in Western culture are misogynist and emotionally repressed, and all women are at ease with emotional intimacy. By encouraging women to produce woman-centered art and literature, psychoanalytic feminism has opened our eyes to the strengths of female bodies and sexualities. But it can lock women artists, musicians, and writers into a categorically female sensibility and emphasize their difference from men and the dominant culture even more. Women's emotional and erotic power is unleashed and made visible in women's cultural productions, but they are separated from men's culture, which is still dominant.

Summary

A culture's symbol system communicates both obvious and subliminal meanings. Ordinary language reflects gender hierarchies in conscious and deliberate devaluation (as in referring to adult women as "girls") and in careless language that renders women invisible (referring to men and women peers as "the guys"). Symbolic language, however, does not just name in ways that praise and denigrate; symbolic language reflects and creates the culture's "unconscious." Psychoanalytic feminism shows how Western culture represents men's fear of women, and dread of emotional involvement, in plays, operas, art, and in movies, rap music, and MTV.

In Freudian theory, gendered personality development comes out of the resolution of the Oedipus complex, in which the young boy represses his emotional attachment to his mother and identifies with his more powerful father because he is afraid that otherwise, like her, he will lose his penis. Western culture is the product of men's fear of losing the phallus, the symbol of masculine power. Since women do not have a penis to lose, they do not participate in the creation of culture.

A little girl continues to be emotionally attached to her mother in the development of her feminine identity. When she grows up, she finds that men cannot fill her emotional needs because they are too detached, and the taboo against homosexuality turns her away from sexual relationships with women. The normal woman, in Freudian theory, will want to mother a child. Her attachment to her child, girl or boy, reproduces the cycle of gendered personality development all over again.

Psychoanalytic feminism's solution to these patterns of gendered personalities and phallic cultural productions is twofold. First, men have to be taught how to be emotionally attached parents to their sons and daughters. With a man as an intimate parent to bond with, a boy will not have to detach emotionally to develop a masculine identity. Second, women have to create art, music, and literature out of their emotional and sexual experiences and their sense of their female bodies. The dominance of the phallus (symbolic masculinity) in Western culture will thus be undermined by the changes in men's unconscious as well as by women's creativity.

Suggested Readings in Psychoanalytic Feminism

Chancer, Lynn S. 1992. *Sadomasochism in Everyday Life: The Dynamics of Power and Powerlessness.* New Brunswick, NJ: Rutgers University Press.

Chodorow, Nancy. 1978. *The Reproduction of Mothering.* Berkeley: University of California Press.

——. 1994. *Femininities, Masculinities, Sexualities: Freud and Beyond.* Lexington: University Press of Kentucky.

Cixous, Hélène, and Catherine Clément. [1975] 1986. *The Newly Born Woman.* (Trans. by Betsy Wing.) Minneapolis: University of Minnesota Press.

Chapter Six ◆ *Psychoanalytic Feminism* 113

Gallop, Jane. 1982. *The Daughter's Seduction: Feminism and Psychoanalysis*. Ithaca, NY: Cornell University Press.

Irigaray, Luce. [1974] 1985. *Speculum of the Other Woman*. (Trans. by Gillian C. Gill). Ithaca, NY: Cornell University Press.

——. [1977] 1985. *This Sex Which Is Not One*. (Trans. by Catherine Porter with Carolyn Burke). Ithaca, NY: Cornell University Press.

Marks, Elaine, and Isabelle de Courtivron (eds.). 1981. *New French Feminisms*. New York: Schocken.

McClary, Susan. 1991. *Feminine Endings: Music, Gender, and Sexuality*. Minneapolis: University of Minnesota Press.

Mitchell, Juliet. 1975. *Psychoanalysis and Feminism*. New York: Vintage.

Mitchell, Juliet, and Jacqueline Rose (eds.). 1985. *Feminine Sexuality: Jacques Lacan and the École Freudienne*. New York: Norton.

Mulvey, Laura. 1989. *Visual and Other Pleasures*. Bloomington: Indiana University Press.

Chapter Seven

Standpoint Feminism

Sources of Gender Inequality

- The neglect of women's perspective and experiences in the production of knowledge
- Women's exclusion from the sciences
- Invisibility of women's perspective in the social sciences

Remedies

- Making women central to research in the physical and social sciences, as researchers and as subjects
- Asking research questions from a woman's point of view

Contributions

- Reframing research questions and priorities
- Challenging the universality of scientific "facts"
- Creating a feminist paradigm for the production of knowledge

Radical, lesbian, and psychoanalytic feminist theories of women's oppression converge in standpoint feminism, which argues that knowledge must be produced from a woman's as well as a man's point of view. The main idea among the gender resistance feminisms is that women's experiences and perspectives should be central, not invisible or marginal, to knowledge, culture, and politics. This idea is the basis for standpoint feminism. Simply put, standpoint feminism says that women's "voices" are different from men's, and they must be heard in the production of knowledge.

Standpoint feminism is a critique of mainstream science and social science, a methodology for feminist research, and an analysis of the power that lies in producing knowledge. The sciences and social sciences are supposed to be universal in their application, but they present the world as it is seen through men's eyes. Men have dominated the production of knowledge in laboratories and in social science research. Standpoint feminism argues that this knowledge is not universal because it is shaped by *men's* views of the world. Women see the world from a different angle, and they are still excluded from much of science. In the social sciences, it is only in the last 20 years that questions have been asked from a woman's point of view. In anthropology, for example, men writing on evolution represented our early primate ancestors as chest-beating, aggressive male gorillas; women in the same field argued that humans were more like the gentler, cooperative male and female chimpanzees.

In the twentieth century, philosophers, psychologists, and physicists have argued that the social location, experiences, and point of view of the investigator or "looker," as well as those of the subjects or the "looked at," interact in producing what we know. A complete picture of a school, for instance, has to include the perspectives of the researcher, the teachers, students, their families, the school administrators, the bureaucrats of the department of education, and the politicians who set the school's budget.

The impact of the everyday world in its experiential reality and the structures that limit, shape, organize, and penetrate it are different for people in different social locations—but especially different for women and men because Western society is so gender-divided. Consider the school again—won't viewpoints be different if the teachers and involved parents are mostly women and the school and departmental administrators and politicians mostly men? Is a man or a woman researcher more likely to see the gendered concentration of power and its impact on curriculum and sports programs? Similarly, in a racially or ethnically divided community, it makes a lot of difference in the way research is done when the researcher is a member of the disadvantaged rather than the advantaged community.

Although men could certainly do research on and about women, and women on men, standpoint feminism argues that women are more sensitive to how other women see problems and set priorities and therefore would be better able to design and conduct research from their point of view. It is not enough, however, to just add more women to research teams or even to have them head a team—these women have to have a feminist viewpoint. They have to be critical of mainstream concepts that justify established lines of power, and they should recognize that "facts" can reflect current values and beliefs about women and men.

A prime example of how assumptions permeate science is the research on sex/gender differences. The research supposedly compares genetically identified females and males (sex differences), but the data come from social behavior (gender differences). In biology, since 1959, the hypothesized source of sex differences has been XX and XY chromosomes, then testosterone and estrogen, and now it is the prenatal "hardwiring" of the brain through genetic and/or hormonal input. Thus, a girl's choice of a career in elementary school teaching and a boy's selection of engineering is attributed to genes, chromosomes, hormones, or brain organization. Socialization, family and peer pressure, the advice of school counselors, and the gender-typing of jobs are omitted from the picture.

Even though there has been experimental evidence since the 1930s that the so-called male and female hormones are equally important to the development of both sexes, and we know from sports competitions that people with XY chromosomes can have female anatomy and physiology, all of the research efforts in this century have been geared to finding clear male–female differences, preferably with an easily identifiable physiological source. Before the intensive criticism of feminist scientists and social scientists, there was very little effort to document the social sources of masculinity and femininity in Western societies. The scientific assumption is still that gender-typed social behavior has to come out of physiological, or hormonal, or genetic, or brain differences because it is so widespread. But any introductory cultural anthropology text has descriptions of assertive women and passive men, of men weaving and women building houses, of women heads of families, and of kinship structures where children belong to the mother's tribe, not the father's.

The dominant status of men varies today and has varied throughout history. The Scandinavian countries are much more egalitarian when it comes to gender than the fundamentalist Islamic countries, yet their women and men presumably have the same kinds of genes, chromosomes, hormones, and brains.

In addition to *phenomenology* (the philosophy that says that what we know comes out of our social location and experience), the grounding for standpoint feminism comes from marxist and socialist feminist theory, which applies Marx's concept of class consciousness to women and men, and from psychoanalytic feminist theory, which describes the gendering of the unconscious. Standpoint feminism argues that as physical and social producers of children—out of bodies, emotions, thought, and sheer physical labor—women are grounded in material reality in ways that men are not. Women are responsible for most of the everyday work, even if they are highly educated, while highly educated men concentrate on the abstract and the intellectual. Because they are closely connected to their bodies and their emotions, women's unconscious as well as conscious view of the world is unitary and concrete. If women produced knowledge, it would be much more in touch with the everyday, material world and with the connectedness among people, because that is what women experience.

In the following excerpt, Nancy Hartsock, one of the first standpoint feminists, defines "standpoint" and describes why a woman's labor makes her way of thinking different from a man's.

The Nature of a Standpoint

Nancy C. M. Hartsock

A standpoint is not simply an interested position (interpreted as bias) but is interested in the sense of being engaged. It is true that a desire to conceal real social relations can contribute to an obscurantist account, and it is also true that the ruling gender and class have material interests in deception. A standpoint, however, carries with it the contention that there are some perspectives on society from which, however well-intentioned one may be, the real relations of humans with each other and with the natural world are not visible. This contention should be sorted into a number of distinct epistemological and political claims: (1) Material life (class position in Marxist theory) not only structures but sets limits on the understanding of social relations. (2) If material life is structured in fundamentally opposing ways for two different groups, one can expect that the vision of each will represent an inversion of the other, and in systems of domination the vision available to the rulers will be both partial and perverse. (3) The vision of the ruling class (or gender) structures the material relations in which all parties are forced to participate, and therefore cannot be dismissed as simply false. (4) In consequence, the vision available to the oppressed group must be struggled for and represents an achievement which requires both science to see beneath the surface of the social relations in which all are forced to participate, and the education which can only grow from struggle to change those relations. (5) As an engaged vision, the understanding of the oppressed, the adoption of a standpoint exposes the real relations among human beings as inhuman, points beyond the present, and carries a historically liberatory role. . . .

The feminist standpoint which emerges through an examination of women's activities is related to the proletarian standpoint, but deeper going. Women and workers inhabit a world in which the emphasis is on change rather than stasis, a world characterized by interaction with natural substances rather than separation from nature, a world in which quality is more important than quantity, a world in which the unification of mind and body is inherent in the activities performed. Yet, there are some important differences, differences marked by the fact that the proletarian (if male) is immersed in this world only during the time his labor power is being used by the capitalist. If, to paraphrase Marx, we follow the worker home from the factory, we can once again perceive a change in the *dramatis personae.* He who before followed behind as the worker, timid and holding back, with nothing to expect but a hiding, now strides in front while a third person, not specifically present in Marx's account of the transaction between capitalist and worker (both of whom are male) follows timidly behind, carrying groceries, baby, and diapers. . . .

Women's activity as institutionalized has a double aspect—their contribution to subsistence, and their contribution to childrearing. Whether or not all of us do both, women as a sex are institutionally responsible for producing both goods and human beings and all women are forced to become the kinds of people who can do both. Although the nature of women's contribution to subsistence varies immensely over time and space, my primary focus here is on capitalism, with a secondary focus on the Western class societies which preceded it. In capitalism, women contribute both production for wages and production of goods in the home, that is, they like men sell their labor power and produce both commodities and surplus value, and produce use-values in the home. Unlike men, however, women's lives are institutionally defined by their production of use-values in the home. And here we begin to encounter the narrowness of the Marxian concept of production. Women's production of use-values in the home has not been well understood by socialists. It is no surprise to feminists that Engels, for example, simply asks how women can continue to do the work in the home and also work in production outside the home. Marx too takes for granted women's responsibility for household labor. He repeats, as if it were his own, the question of a Belgian factory inspector: If a mother works for wages, "how will [the household's] internal economy be cared for; who will look after the young children; who will get ready the meals, do the washing and mending?"

Let us trace both the outlines and the consequences of woman's dual contribution to subsistence in capitalism. Women's labor, like that of the male worker, is contact with material necessity. Their contribution to subsistence, like that of the male worker, involves them in a world in which the relation to nature and to concrete human requirements is central, both in the form of interaction with natural substances whose quality, rather than quantity, is important to the production of meals, clothing, etc., and in the form of close attention to the natural changes in these substances. Women's labor both for wages and even more in household production involves a unification of mind and body for the purpose of transforming natural substances into socially defined goods. This too is true of the labor of the male worker.

There are, however, important differences. First, women as a group work more than men. We are all familiar with the phenomenon of the "double day," and with indications that women work many more hours per week than men. Second, a larger proportion of women's labor time is devoted to the production of use values than men's. Only some of the goods women produce are commodities (however much they live in a society structured by commodity production and exchange). Third, women's production is structured by repetition in a different way than men's. While repetition for both the woman and the male worker may take the form of production of the same object, over and over—whether apple pies or brake linings—women's work in housekeeping involves a repetitious cleaning.

Thus, the male worker in the process of production, is involved in contact with necessity, and interchange with nature as well as with other human beings but the process of production or work does not consume his whole life. The activity of a woman in the home as well as the work she does for wages keeps her continually in contact with a world of qualities and change. Her immersion in the world of use—in concrete, many-qualitied, changing material processes—is more complete than his. And if life itself consists of sensuous activity, the vantage point available to women on the basis of their contribution to subsistence represents an intensification and deepening of the materialist world view and consciousness available to the producers of commodities in capitalism, an intensification of class consciousness. The availability of this outlook to even non-working-class women has been strikingly formulated by Marilyn French in *The Women's Room.*

> Washing the toilet used by three males, and the floor and walls around it, is, Mira thought, coming face to face with necessity. And that is why women were saner than men, did not come up with the mad, absurd schemes men developed; they were in touch with necessity, they had to wash the toilet bowl and floor.

The focus on women's subsistence activity rather than men's leads to a model in which the capitalist (male) lives a life structured completely by commodity exchange and not at all by production, and at the furthest distance from contact with concrete material life. The male worker marks a way station on the path to the other extreme of the constant contact with material necessity in women's contribution to subsistence. There are, of course important differences along the lines of race and class. For example, working class men seem to do more domestic labor than men higher up in the class structure—car repairs, carpentry, etc. And until very recently, the wage work done by most women of color replicated the housework required by their own households. Still, there are commonalities present in the institutionalized sexual division of labor which make women responsible for both housework and wage work.

The female contribution to subsistence, however, represents only a part of women's labor. Women also produce/reproduce men (and other women) on both a daily and a longterm basis. This aspect of women's "production" exposes the deep inadequacies of the concept of production as a description of women's activity. One does not (cannot) produce another human being in anything like the way one produces an object such as a chair. Much more is involved, activity which cannot easily be dichotomized into play or work. Helping another to develop, the gradual relinquishing of control, the experience of the human limits of one's action—all these are important features of women's activity as mothers. Women as mothers even more than as workers, are institutionally involved in processes of change and growth, and more than workers, must understand the importance of avoiding excessive control in order to help others grow. The activity involved is far more complex than the instrumental working with others to transform objects. (Interestingly, much of women's wage work—nursing, social work, and some secretarial jobs in particular—requires and depends on the relational and interpersonal skills women learned by being mothered by someone of the same sex.)

This aspect of women's activity too is not without consequences. Indeed, it is in the production of men by women and the appropriation of this labor and women themselves by men that the opposition between feminist and masculinist experience and outlook is rooted, and it is here that features of the proletarian vision are enhanced and modified for the woman and diluted for the man. The female experience in reproduction represents a unity with nature which goes beyond the proletarian experience of interchange with nature. . . .

Reprinted from: Nancy C. M. Hartsock, "The Feminist Standpoint: Developing the Ground for a Specific Feminist Historical Materialism," in *Feminism and Methodology*, edited by Sandra Harding, pp. 159–60, 164–66. Copyright © 1987 by Indiana University Press. Reprinted by permission.

Standpoint feminism is arguing for more than equal representation of all viewpoints. There is a power issue here as well. Whoever sets the agendas for scientific research, shapes the content of education, chooses the symbols that permeate cultural productions, and decides political priorities has *hegemonic power*. *Hegemony* is the value base that legitimates a society's unquestioned assumptions. In Western society, the justifications for many of our ideas about women and men come from science. We believe in scientific "facts" and rarely question their objectivity. That is why standpoint feminism puts so much emphasis on demonstrating that scientific knowledge produced mostly by men is not universal and general but partial and particular.

But is all men's and women's experience the same? Is not all knowledge partial? Race, ethnicity, religion, social class, age, and sexual orientation are also social locations. They intersect with gender to produce varied life experiences and outlooks. There may be a common core to women's experiences, perhaps because they share similar bodies, but standpoint feminism cannot ignore the input from social characteristics that are as important as gender. All men may be dominant over the women of their group, but some are certainly subordinate to other men.

In a paper that was a commentary on Sandra Harding's groundbreaking *The Science Question in Feminism* (see Suggested Readings), Donna Haraway proposes a way out of the dilemma of reconciling woman's standpoint with differences in women's life experiences. She says that all knowledge is situated, just as standpoint feminism claims, but that situations differ, and so do all perspectives. Truths, therefore, must be partial. This diversity is a strength, not a weakness, in feminism.

THE PRIVILEGE OF PARTIAL PERSPECTIVES

Donna Haraway

. . . Feminism loves another science: the sciences and politics of interpretation, translation, stuttering, and the partly understood. Feminism is about the sciences of the multiple subject with (at least) double vision. Feminism is about a critical vision consequent upon a critical positioning in unhomogeneous gendered social space. Translation is always interpretive, critical, and partial. Here is a ground for conversation, rationality, and objectivity—which is power-sensitive, not pluralist, "conversation." It is not even the mythic cartoons of physics and mathematics—incorrectly caricatured in antiscience ideology as exact, hypersimple knowledges—that have come to represent the hostile other to feminist paradigmatic models of scientific knowledge, but the dreams of the perfectly known in high-technology, permanently militarized scientific productions and positionings, the god trick of a Star Wars paradigm of rational knowledge. So location is about vulnerability; location resists the politics of closure, finality, or to borrow from Althusser, feminist objectivity resists "simplification in the last instance." That is because feminist embodiment resists fixation and is insatiably curious about the webs of differential positioning. There is no single feminist standpoint because our maps require too many dimensions for that metaphor to ground our visions. But the feminist standpoint theorists' goal of an epistemology and politics of engaged, accountable positioning remains eminently potent. The goal is better accounts of the world, that is, "science."

Above all, rational knowledge does not pretend to disengagement: to be from everywhere and so nowhere, to be free from interpretation, from being represented, to be fully self-contained or fully formalizable. Rational knowledge is a process of ongoing critical interpretation among "fields" of interpreters and decoders. Rational knowledge is power-sensitive conversation. Decoding and transcoding plus translation and criticism; all are necessary. So science becomes the paradigmatic model, not of closure, but of that which is contestable and contested. Science becomes the myth, not of what escapes human agency and responsibility in a realm above the fray, but, rather, of accountability and responsibility for translations and solidarities linking the cacophonous visions and visionary voices that characterize the knowledges of the subjugated. A splitting of senses, a confusion of voice and sight, rather than clear and distinct ideas, becomes the metaphor for the ground of the rational. We seek not the knowledges ruled by phallogocentrism (nostalgia for the presence of the one true Word) and disembodied vision. We seek those ruled by partial sight and limited voice—not partiality for its own sake but, rather, for the sake of the connections and unexpected openings situated knowledges make possible. Situated knowledges are about communities, not about isolated individuals. The only way to find a larger vision is to be somewhere in particular. The science question in feminism is about objectivity as positioned rationality. Its images are not the products of escape and transcendence of limits (the view from above) but the joining of partial views and halting voices into a collective subject position that promises a vision of the means of ongoing finite embodiment, of living within limits and contradictions—of views from somewhere.

Critique. A woman-centered perspective is a needed corrective to a gender-blind neutralism that erases women's experience. But the exclusive focus on "woman" is troublesome. Are women so much alike that they can be expected to always have similar experiences and a unitary perspective? Does standpoint feminism create a universal Woman who is actually middle-class, Western, heterosexual, and White? Does this universal Woman suppress other women's voices? How can they be heard? For that matter, don't men also differ by race, ethnicity, religion, social class, and sexual orientation?

Cultural feminism's answer to the diversity-sameness issue is that what binds all women together is their bodies and their connectedness to people through their ties to their mothers and their nurturing abilities. A strong critique of this view focuses on these claims of essential differences between men and women and the promotion of a separate and distinctive woman's culture rooted in female bodies. Many feminists feel that these views are a throwback to biological justifications of women's inferiority. The same criticism can be applied to standpoint feminism and its privileging of women's bodily experiences in the production of knowledge.

However, if women's standpoint is not located in the female body but in women's place in a gendered social order that is secondary and constantly threatened by violence, rape, and sexual harassment, then we can speak of a shared woman's standpoint without reverting to a direct biological cause. Standpoint feminism can legitimately argue that women's bodies are the source of their sexual oppression because of the ways they are used and abused by men, and that their consciousness is shaped by their family role as the primary parent. Women's bodies are not erased but are mediated by social processes.

Similarly, it is not male biology that makes men dominant but their social power, which they get because they have a visible mark of identity that sets them off from women—a penis. Men in diverse social circumstances have something in common—the privileges of dominant status. (Its *symbol* is the *phallus*.) Social locations and experiences, such as growing up a girl or a boy in a poor Black community, create particular women's and men's identities and standpoints. These shared particular identities are like concentric circles within the larger circle of womanhood and manhood. Both the common and the diverse ways of thinking are needed for fully representative knowledge.

Summary

Standpoint feminism claims that what people think is universal, objective knowledge is biased because it does not include the life experiences of those who are not members of the dominant group. It challenges the claim that what is represented as "fact" is applicable to everyone. Phenomenologists and perception psychologists have argued that knowledge is produced out of experience. If that is so, then knowledge produced without women's experiences is not applicable to the universe but only to half of it. In order to balance out the dominance of men's experiences in most knowledge production, standpoint feminism elevates *women's experience*.

Using marxist, socialist, and psychoanalytic feminisms' analyses of how women's lives and work shape their conscious and unconscious thinking, standpoint feminism says that women's people-oriented perspective must be used in producing knowledge.

We think that science is detached from the particulars of everyday life. That is not even true of astronomy and physics, which have a social impact in space travel and nuclear power, but it is especially false when it comes to research on people. When we want to know what makes people think and act the way they do, we are using the data of everyday life. The lives of women and of men of diverse races, ethnicities, religions, social classes, and sexual orientations must be part of these data.

Standpoint feminism challenges the sciences and social sciences to take a more critical view of their basic assumptions, especially about women and men. It criticizes the research on sex/gender differences because women's social and experiential reality are ignored. Standpoint feminism claims that the search for clearly identifiable biological markers of sex differences is a search for the legitimation of the gendered status quo. Modern Western societies today believe in science as an explanation for the way things are; past generations believed life circumstances were God-given. Standpoint feminism claims that when it comes to sex and gender, there is more faith than fact in men's science.

Suggested Readings in Standpoint Feminism

Alcoff, Linda, and Elizabeth Potter (eds.). 1993. *Feminist Epistemologies*. New York and London: Routledge.

Belenkey, Mary Field et al. (eds.). 1986. *Women's Ways of Knowing: The Development of Self, Voice, and Mind*. New York: Basic Books.

Embree, Lester, and Linda Fisher (eds.). Forthcoming. *Feminism and Phenomenology*. Dordrecht and Boston: Kluwer.

Goldberger, Nancy Rule et al. (eds.). 1996. *Knowledge, Difference, and Power: Essays Inspired by Women's Ways of Knowing.* New York: Basic Books.

Haraway, Donna. 1989. *Primate Visions.* New York and London: Routledge.

Harding, Sandra. 1986. *The Science Question in Feminism.* Ithaca, NY: Cornell University Press.

——. 1991. *Whose Science? Whose Knowledge? Thinking from Women's Lives.* Ithaca, NY: Cornell University Press.

Keller, Evelyn Fox. 1985. *Reflections on Gender and Science.* New Haven, CT: Yale University Press.

Laslett, Barbara, Sally Gregory Kohlstedt, Helen Longino, and Evelynn Hammonds (eds.). 1996. *Gender and Scientific Authority.* Chicago: University of Chicago Press.

Levesque-Lopman, Louise. 1988. *Claiming Reality: Phenomenology and Women's Experience.* Totowa, NJ: Rowman & Littlefield.

Smith, Dorothy E. 1987. *The Everyday World as Problematic.* Toronto: University of Toronto Press.

——. 1990. *The Conceptual Practices of Power: A Feminist Sociology of Knowledge.* Toronto: University of Toronto Press.

——. 1990. *Texts, Facts, and Femininity: Exploring the Relations of Ruling.* New York and London: Routledge.

Van den Wijngaard, Marianne. 1997. *Reinventing the Sexes: The Biomedical Construction of Femininity and Masculinity.* Bloomington: Indiana University Press.

Part IV

GENDER REBELLION FEMINISMS

Overview

Gender rebellion feminisms have long roots in historical, political, social psychological, and cultural studies. Since the late 1980s, they have become major perspectives, amounting to what some have called *third-wave feminisms*. They address the limits of gender resistance feminisms, especially the problems of the unity of women, the privileged perspective of women's standpoint, and the source of identity in identity politics. They are also part of the postmodern questioning of assumptions underlying what we think and believe.

Multiracial feminism, whose roots are in Black history and politics, argues that the major social statuses of a society produce a complex hierarchical stratification system. By teasing out multiple strands of oppression and exploitation, multiracial feminism shows that gender, race, and ethnicity are intertwined social structures: How people are gendered depends on whether they are members of dominant or subordinate racial and ethnic groups. Social class is also an especially crucial dimension, given the wide differences between the poor and the rich throughout the world.

Multiracial feminism (which can equally well be called multiethnic or multicultural feminism) creates theories and politics of gender inequality that interweave the subordinate status of gender with the continuum of dominance and subordination of other social statuses. It argues that feminist political activism can no longer be based only on gender but must consider race, ethnicity, and social class as well. Thus, African American women have developed a "womanist" rather than a feminist approach. The battle for rights and dignity includes men, but women's perspectives and cultural contributions are made visible as well.

Men's feminism, drawing on marxist analyses of social class, has focused on the interlocking structures of power that make one group of men dominant and rank everyone else in a complex hierarchy of privilege and disadvantage. It documents the gender practices that both exclude women from competition with men and determine which men are able to attain positions of great power. The culture of violence in many Western societies and its enactment in sports has come under criticism by men's feminism. Race, ethnicity, religion, social class, and sexual orientation are additional dimensions that men's feminism uses in its analyses of men's social statuses.

In many ways, men's feminism and multiracial feminism are producing parallel data about the ways gender inequality plays itself out within and between different social groups of women and men. One focuses on men and the other on women, but in their overall perspective, they are talking about gender as part of the structure of power and privilege that affects the lives of women and men of all different groups.

Social construction feminism comes out of symbolic interaction in social psychology, which shows how people construct multiple meanings and indentities in their daily encounters. Social construction feminism analyzes the general processes that create what we perceive to be the differences between women and men. These processes also construct racial and ethnic stereotypes and beliefs about homosexuality as contrasted with heterosexuality. They impose categorical divisions on physiological and behavioral continuums and use visible markers, such as skin color or penis, as signs of supposedly inborn and essential characteristics. Because these physiological markers are usually hidden (people do not walk on the streets naked) and varied (some African Americans have pale skin), other identifiers of social status are needed: Clothing, jewelry, and hair styles are the most common. In face-to-face encounters, visible cues of gender, class, ethnicity, and so on, pattern subsequent behavior. (They act like team colors.) Evident differences within categories of people and similarities between groups are repressed or ignored.

Social construction feminism argues that multiple categories would better reflect the variety in people, but the gendered social order is built on a binary division of labor that needs clearly differentiated categories of women and men who can be assigned to gender-typed roles in the family, jobs in the workforce, and positions in government, the professions, and the arts.

Postmodern feminism and queer theory, located for the most part in cultural studies, challenge conventional binary oppositions even more. They claim that gender and sexuality are performances, and that individuals modify their displays of masculinity and femininity to suit their own purposes. Males can easily masquerade as women, and females can pass for men. Like clothing, sexuality and gender can be put on. Indeed, the exaggerations and parodies of gender by performers such as Michael Jackson and Madonna show how much manliness and womanliness are "put ons."

Gender rebellion feminisms' theories destabilize what many people think is normal and natural and moral, but they have only begun to develop new practices for work, family life, and intimate relationships. They need to translate multiple categories into everyday living, which could be revolutionary enough. But to fulfill their political potential, these feminisms need to spell out what precisely has to be done in all the institutions and organizations of a society—family, workplace, government, the arts, religion, and so on—to ensure equal participation and opportunity for every person in every group.

Chapter Eight

Multiracial Feminism

Sources of Gender Inequality

- The intersection of racial, ethnic, class, and gender discrimination
- Continued patterns of disadvantage built into the social structure
- Cultural devaluation of women and men of subordinated racial and ethnic groups

Remedies

- Equal access to education, good jobs, and political power
- Science and other knowledge production that reflects the subordinate group's perspectives
- Cultural productions by women and men of varied racial and ethnic heritages

Contributions

- Analysis of multiple, intertwined systems of oppression
- Development of a complex politics of identity
- *Womanist* and *subaltern* fiction, poetry, art, music, crafts—cultural productions from the perspective of the "other"

Coming in a long line of critical theory and activist politics, multi-racial feminism (sometimes called multiethnic or multicultural feminism) focuses on the *intersectionality* of gender race, ethnicity, and social class. It argues that you cannot look at one of these social statuses alone, nor can you add them one after another. Their interaction is synergistic: together they construct a social location. Some locations are more oppressive than others because they are the result of *multiple systems of domination.*

Gender, race, ethnicity, and social class comprise a complex hier-archical stratification system in the United States, in which upper-class, White men and women oppress lower-class women and men of disad-vantaged races, ethnicities, and religions. In teasing out the multiple strands of oppression and exploitation, multiracial feminism has shown that gender is intertwined with and cannot be separated from race, ethnicity, and social class. Race, ethnicity, and social class, however, are continuums of advantage and disadvantage, but gender is a dichotomy. Thus, the social location of a man and woman of the same racial, ethnic, or social class status differs. Men of the subordinate group may be as oppressed as the women but often in different ways. For example, Black men in the United States are rewarded for success in boxing and football, but are punished for violent behavior outside the sports arena; Black women are hired to take care of White children but are stigma-tized for having many children of their own.

A woman member of a disadvantaged group may not be more disadvantaged than the man: in some economies, she may be able to get a job and a man may be out of work. Ironically, the lower on the social ladder a group is, the more likely are the women and men to be equal. That is because there are few resources for the men to monop-olize. As a group gains advantages, such as the chance for higher education, the men usually advance over the women.

There is a different social map for the men and the women of the same racial or ethnic group, just as there is a different social map for Whites and "others." There is also a different social map for the very wealthy, the rich, the middle income, the "just bill-payers" and those who scrape together a variety of survival sources. But if you made one map that included everyone, you would find clusters and patterns: the wealthy are mostly White men and the survivors mostly women of color; disadvantaged racial and ethnic groups and women are more numerous at the bottom of the hierarchy. Thus, your overall social status is a location in a social structure.

Not only life chances, but values, identity, and consciousness of self are rooted in all the major social categories; they are the walls and windows of our lives—combined, they structure what we experience, do, feel, see, and ultimately believe about ourselves and others. Multiracial feminism therefore talks of the outlooks and behavior of Black working-class women and Black working-class men, wealthy White women and wealthy White men, middle-class Latinas and middle-class Latinos, poor Chinese women and poor Chinese men, and so on.

The most advantaged group's values and ideas about the way people should behave usually dominate policies and social agendas. Multiracial feminism's politics focuses on this issue, especially with regard to the family. If the White, middle-class, two-parent family is taken as the norm, then the Black extended family of grandmothers, mothers, aunts, and "othermothers"—all responsible for the children of the household and pooling resources—is a deviant or problem family that needs changing. Health care is another area where the dominant group's perspective translates into allocation of resources. If psychological stress is defined as resulting from pressure in a high-powered job, then the pressures of living in a ghetto are ignored.

The following excerpt by two sociologists who have done extensive research on race, ethnicity, and gender, lays out the structural premises of multiracial feminism.

WHAT IS MULTIRACIAL FEMINISM?

Maxine Baca Zinn and Bonnie Thornton Dill

A new set of feminist theories have emerged from the challenges put forth by women of color. Multiracial feminism is an evolving body of theory and practice informed by wide-ranging intellectual traditions. This framework does not offer a singular or unified feminism but a body of knowledge situating women and men in multiple systems of domination. U.S. multiracial feminism encompasses several emergent perspectives developed primarily by women of color: African Americans, Latinas, Asian Americans, and Native Americans, women whose analyses are shaped by their unique perspectives as "outsiders within"—marginal intellectuals whose social locations provide them with a particular perspective on self and society. Although U.S. women of color represent many races and ethnic backgrounds—with different histories and cultures—our feminisms cohere in their treatment of race as a basic social division, a structure of power, a focus of political struggle, and hence a fundamental force in shaping women's and men's lives. . . .

We use "multiracial" rather than "multicultural" as a way of underscoring race as a power system that interacts with other structured inequalities to shape genders. Within the U. S. context, race, and the system of meanings and ideologies which accompany it, is a fundamental organizing principle of social relationships. Race affects all women and men, although in different ways. Even cultural and group differences among women are produced through interaction within a racially stratified social order. Therefore, although we do not discount the importance of culture, we caution that cultural analytic frameworks that ignore race tend to view women's differences as the product of group-specific values and practices that often result in the marginalization of cultural groups which are then perceived as exotic expressions of a normative center. Our focus on race stresses the social construction of differently situated social groups and their varying degrees of advantage and power. Additionally, this emphasis on race takes on increasing political importance in an era where discourse about race is governed by color-evasive language and a preference for individual rather than group remedies for social inequalities. Our analyses insist upon the primary and pervasive nature of race in contemporary U.S. society while at the same time acknowledging how race both shapes and is shaped by a variety of other social relations.

In the social sciences, multiracial feminism grew out of socialist feminist thinking. Theories about how political economic forces shape women's lives were influential as we began to uncover the social causes of racial ethnic women's subordination. But socialist feminism's concept of capitalist patriarchy, with its focus on women's unpaid (reproductive) labor in the home failed to address racial differences in the organization of reproductive labor. As feminists of color have argued, "reproductive labor has divided along racial as well as gender lines, and the specific-characteristics have varied regionally and changed over time as capitalism has reorganized" (Glenn 1992). Despite the limitations of socialist feminism, this body of literature has been especially useful in pursuing questions about the interconnections among systems of domination.

Race and ethnic studies was the other major social scientific source of multiracial feminism. It provided a basis for comparative analyses of groups that are socially and legally subordinated and remain culturally distinct within U.S. society. This includes the systematic discrimination of socially constructed racial groups and their distinctive cultural arrangements. Historically, the categories of African American, Latino, Asian American, and Native American were constructed as both racially and culturally distinct. Each group has a distinctive culture, shares a common heritage, and has developed a common identity within a larger society that subordinates them.

We recognize, of course, certain problems inherent in an uncritical use of the multiracial label. First, the perspective can be hampered by a biracial model in which only African Americans and whites are seen as racial categories and all other groups are viewed through the prism of cultural differences. Latinos and Asians have always occupied distinctive places within the racial hierarchy, and current shifts in the composition of the U.S. population are racializing these groups anew.

A second problem lies in treating multiracial feminism as a single analytical framework, and its principle architects, women of color, as an undifferentiated category. The concepts "multiracial feminism," "racial ethnic women," and "women of color" "homogenize quite different experiences and can falsely universalize experiences across race, ethnicity, sexual orientation, and age" (Andersen and Collins 1992, xvi). The feminisms created by women of color exhibit a plurality of intellectual and political positions. We speak in many voices, with inconsistencies that are born of our different social locations. Multiracial feminism embodies this plurality and richness. Our intent is not to falsely universalize women of color. Nor do we wish to promote a new racial essentialism in place of the old gender essentialism. Instead, we use these concepts to examine the structures and experiences produced by intersecting forms of race and gender.

It is also essential to acknowledge that race is a shifting and contested category whose meanings construct definitions of all aspects of social life. In the United States it helped define citizenship by excluding everyone who was not a white, male property owner. It defined labor as slave or free, coolie or contract, and family as available only to those men whose marriages were recognized or whose wives could immigrate with them. Additionally, racial meanings are contested both within groups and between them.

Although definitions of race are at once historically and geographically specific, they are also transnational, encompassing diasporic groups and crossing traditional geographic boundaries. Thus, while U.S. multiracial feminism calls attention to the fundamental importance of race, it must also locate the meaning of race within specific national traditions.

The Distinguishing Features of Multiracial Feminism

By attending to these problems, multiracial feminism offers a set of analytic premises for thinking about and theorizing gender. The following themes distinguish this branch of feminist inquiry.

First, multiracial feminism asserts that gender is constructed by a range of interlocking inequalities, what Patricia Hill Collins calls a "matrix of domination" (1990). The idea of a matrix is that several fundamental systems work with and through each other. People experience race, class, gender, and sexuality differently depending upon their social location in the structures of race, class, gender, and sexuality. For example, people of the same race will experience race differently depending upon their location in the class structure as working class, professional managerial class, or unemployed; in the gender structure as female or male; and in structures of sexuality as heterosexual, homosexual, or bisexual.

Multiracial feminism also examines the simultaneity of systems in shaping women's experience and identity. Race, class, gender, and sexuality are not reducible to individual attributes to be measured and assessed for their separate contribution in explaining given social outcomes, an approach that Elizabeth Spelman calls "popbead metaphysics," where a woman's identity consists of the sum of parts neatly divisible from one another (1988, 136). The matrix of domination seeks to account for the multiple ways that women experience themselves as gendered, raced, classed, and sexualized.

Second, multiracial feminism emphasizes the intersectional nature of hierarchies at all levels of social life. Class, race, gender, and sexuality are components of both social structure and social interaction. Women and men are differently embedded in locations created by these cross-cutting hierarchies. As a result, women and men throughout the social order experience different forms of privilege and subordination, depending on their race, class, gender, and sexuality. In other words, intersecting forms of domination produce *both* oppression *and* opportunity. At the same time that structures of race, class, and gender create disadvantages for women of color, they provide unacknowledged benefits for those who are at the top of these hierarchies—whites, members of the upper classes, and males. Therefore, multiracial feminism applies not only to racial ethnic women but also to women and men of all races, classes, and genders.

Third, multiracial feminism highlights the relational nature of dominance and subordination. Power is the cornerstone of women's differences. This means that women's differences are *connected* in systematic ways. Race is a vital element in the pattern of relations among minority and white women. . . .

Fourth, multiracial feminism explores the interplay of social structure and women's agency. Within the constraints of race, class, and gender oppression, women create viable lives for themselves, their families, and their communities. Women of color have resisted and often undermined the forces of power that control them. From acts of quiet dignity and steadfast determination to involvement in revolt and rebellion, women struggle to shape their own lives. Racial oppression has been a common focus of the "dynamic of oppositional agency" of women of color (Mohanty 1991, 13). . . .

Fifth, multiracial feminism encompasses wide-ranging methodological approaches, and like other branches of feminist thought, relies on varied theoretical tools as well. . . . In the last decade, the opening up of academic feminism has focused attention on social location in the production of knowledge. Most basically, research by and about marginalized women has destabilized what used to be considered as universal categories of gender. Marginalized locations are well suited for grasping social relations that remained obscure from more privileged vantage points. Lived experience, in other words, creates alternative ways of understanding the social world and the experience of different groups of women within it. Racially informed standpoint epistemologies have provided new topics, fresh questions, and new understandings of women and men. . . .

Sixth, multiracial feminism brings together understandings drawn from the lived experiences of diverse and continuously changing groups of women. Among Asian Americans, Native Americans, Latinas, and Blacks are many different national cultural and ethnic groups. Each one is engaged in the process of testing, refining, and reshaping these broader categories in its own image. Such internal differences heighten awareness of and sensitivity to both commonalities and differences, serving as a constant reminder of the importance of comparative study and maintaining a creative tension between diversity and universalization. . . .

References

Andersen, Margaret L. and Patricia Hill Collins (eds.). *Race, Class and Gender: An Anthology.* Belmont, CA: Wadsworth.

Collins, Patricia Hill. 1990. See Suggested Readings.

Glenn, Evelyn Nakano. 1992. "From Servitude to Service Work: Historical Continuities in the Racial Division of Paid Reproductive Labor." *Signs* 18:1-43.

Mohanty, Chandra Talpade. 1991. See Suggested Readings.

Spelman, Elizabeth. 1988. *Inessential Woman: Problems of Exclusion in Feminist Thought.* Boston: Beacon Press.

For both women and men, the dominant group sets the standards for what behavior is valued, what faces and bodies are considered beautiful, what cultural productions represent "everybody." The subordinate group is always less influential unless it can turn the dominant values upside down, as standpoint feminism does when it says women's values and experiences have to be given as much credit as men's. Multiracial feminism takes the standpoint perspective a step further. It is not enough to dissect a social institution or area of social thought from a woman's point of view; the viewpoint has to include the experiences of women of different racial and ethnic groups and must also take into consideration social class and local economic conditions.

Eating disorders are a case in point. Among young White women, anorexia and bulimia are usually attributed to a desire for a thin, sexually attractive body because there is a culture of thinness in Western societies. For some African American and Hispanic women, however, binge eating and purging are ways of coping with the traumas of their lives—sexual abuse, poverty, racism, and injustice. In all these cases, the underlying cause of the eating disorder is social pressure, but the pressures differ enormously.

As Patricia Hill Collins, one of the major theorists of Black feminism points out in a recent critique of standpoint theory, these experiences are not individual but common to the members of a *group*; thus, they are a vital source of both a world view and a sense of identity. When a group's experiences frame the production of knowledge and culture and set political agendas, that group has power. Most racial and ethnic groups in a heterogeneous society do not have such power; their experiential life-world views do not become part of the mainstream.

WHERE'S THE POWER?

Patricia Hill Collins

. . . First, the notion of a standpoint refers to historically shared, *group-based* experiences. Groups have a degree of permanence over time such that group realities transcend individual experiences. For example, African Americans as a stigmatized racial group existed long before I was born and will probably continue long after I die. While my individual experiences with institutionalized racism will be unique, the types of opportunities and constraints that I encounter on a daily basis will resemble those confronting African Americans as a group. Arguing that Blacks as a group come into being or disappear on the basis of my participation seems narcissistic, egocentric, and archetypally postmodern. In contrast, standpoint theory places less emphasis on individual experiences within socially constructed groups than on the social conditions that construct such groups.

I stress this difference between the individual and the group as units of analysis because using these two constructs as if they were interchangeable clouds understanding of a host of topics, in this case, the very notion of a group-based standpoint. Individualism continues as a taproot in Western theorizing, including feminist versions. Whether bourgeois liberalism positing notions of individual rights or postmodern social theory's celebration of human differences, market-based choice models grounded in individualism argue that freedom exists via the absence of constraints of all sorts, including those of mandatory group membership. Freedom occurs when individuals have rights of mobility in and out of groups, much as we join clubs and other voluntary associations.

But the individual as proxy for the group becomes particularly problematic because standpoint theory's treatment of the group is not synonymous with a "family resemblance" of individual choice expanded to the level of voluntary group association. The notion of standpoint refers to groups having shared histories based on their shared location in relations of power—standpoints arise neither from crowds of individuals nor from groups analytically created by scholars or bureaucrats. Take, for example, the commonality of experiences that emerges from long-standing patterns of racial segregation in the United States. The degree of racial segregation between Blacks and Whites as *groups* is routinely underestimated. Blacks and Whites live in racially segregated neighborhoods, and this basic feature generates distinctive experiences in schools, recreational facilities, shopping areas, health-care systems, and occupational opportunities. Moreover, middle-class Blacks have not been exempt from the effects of diminished opportunities that accompany racial segregation and group discrimination. It is common location within hierarchical power relations that creates groups, not the results of collective decision making of the individuals within the groups. Race, gender, social class, ethnicity, age, and sexuality are not descriptive categories of identity applied to individuals. Instead, these elements of social structure emerge as fundamental devices that foster inequality resulting in groups. . . .

What we now have is increasing sophistication about how to discuss group location, not in the singular social class framework proposed by Marx, nor in the early feminist frameworks arguing the primacy of gender, but within constructs of multiplicity residing in social structures themselves and not in individual women. Fluidity does not mean that groups themselves disappear, to be replaced by an accumulation of decontexualized, unique women whose complexity erases politics. Instead, the fluidity of boundaries operates as a new lens that potentially deepens understanding of how the actual mechanisms of institutional power can change dramatically while continuing to reproduce long-standing inequalities of race, gender, and class that result in group stability. In this sense, group history and location can be seen as points of convergence within hierarchical, multiple, and changing structural power relations.

A second feature of standpoint theory concerns the commonality of experiences and perspectives that emerge for groups differentially arrayed within hierarchical power relations. Keep in mind that if the group has been theorized away, there can be no common experiences or perspectives. Standpoint theory argues that groups who share common placement in hierarchical power relations also share common experiences in such power relations. Such shared angles of vision lead those in similar social locations to be predisposed to interpret these experiences in a comparable fashion. The existence of the group as the unit of analysis neither means that all individuals within the group have the same experiences nor that they interpret them in the same way. Using the group as the focal point provides space for individual agency. While these themes remain meritorious, they simply do not lie at the center of standpoint theory as a theory of group power and the knowledges that group location and power generate.

Unfortunately, the much-deserved attention to issues of individual agency and diversity often overshadow investigating the continued salience of group-based experiences. But group-based experience, especially that of race and/or social class, continues to matter. For example, African American male rates of incarceration in American jails and prisons remain the highest in the world, exceeding even those of South Africa. Transcending social class, region of residence, command of English, ethnic background, or other markers of difference, all Black men must in some way grapple with the actual or potential treatment by the criminal justice system. Moreover, as mothers, daughters, wives, and lovers of Black men, Black women also participate in this common experience. Similarly, children from poor communities and homeless families are unlikely to attend college, not because they lack talent, but because they lack opportunity. Whatever their racial/ethnic classification, poor people as a group confront similar barriers for issues of basic survival. In this sense, standpoint theory seems especially suited to explaining relations of race and/or social class because these systems of power share similar institutional structures. Given the high degree of residential and occupational segregation separating Black and/or working-class groups from White middle-class realities, it becomes plausible to generate arguments about working-class and/or Black culture that emerge from long-standing shared experiences. For both class and race, a much clearer case of a group standpoint can be constructed. Whether individuals from or associated with these groups accept or reject these histories, they recognize the saliency of the notion of group standpoint.

But gender raises different issues, for women are distributed across these other groups. In contrast to standpoints that must learn to accommodate differences within, feminist standpoints must be constructed across differences such as these. Thus, gender represents a distinctly different intellectual and political project within standpoint theory. How effectively can a standpoint theory that was originally developed to explicate the wage exploitation and subsequent impoverishment of European, working- class populations be applied to the extremely heterogeneous population of women in the contemporary United States, let alone globally? For example, Black women and White women do not live in racially integrated women's communities, separated from men and children by processes such as gender steering into such communities, experience bank redlining that results in refusal to lend money to women's communities, attend inferior schools as a result of men moving to all-male suburban areas, and the like. Instead, Black and White women live in racially segregated communities, and the experiences they garner in such communities reflect the racial politics operating overall. Moreover, proximity in physical space is not necessarily the same as occupying a common location in the space of hierarchical power relations. For example, Black women and women of color routinely share academic office space with middle-class and/or White women academics. It is quite common for women of color to clean the office of the feminist academic writing the latest treatise on standpoint theory. While these women occupy the same physical space—this is why proximity should not be confused with group solidarity—they occupy fundamentally different locations in hierarchical power relations. These women did not just enter this space in a random fashion. An entire arsenal of social institutions collectively created paths in which the individuals assigned to one group received better housing, health care, education, and recreational facilities, while those relegated to the other group did with worse or did without. The accumulation of these different experiences led the two groups of women to that same academic space. The actual individuals matter less than the accumulation of social structures that lead to these outcomes. In this sense, developing a political theory for women involves confronting a different and more complex set of issues than that facing race theories or class-based theories because women's inequality is structured differently. . . .

Reprinted from: Patricia Hill Collins, "Comment on Hekman's 'Truth and Method: Feminist Standpoint Theory Revisited': Where's the Power?" in *Signs* 22:375-79. Copyright © 1997 by The University of Chicago Press. Reprinted by permission.

Although multiracial feminism's emphasis is on structural oppression, it also recognizes the multiplicity of cultural identities within all the larger racial and ethnic groups. In the United States, some Whites identify themselves with the home country of their ancestors—Italian, Irish, or another. Some Blacks identify with their African heritage, some with their Jamaican or Haitian backgrounds. Hispanics are from Puerto Rico, from the different South and Central American countries, as well as from Spain. Asians are Chinese, Japanese, Korean, Thai, Laotian, or Vietnamese. Native American cultures are not all the same. India, Pakistan, Bangladesh, and Nepal all have different cultures.

Multiracial feminism has made a political statement out of women's culture within these cultures. What women produce in everyday life, it claims as art: quilts, folk songs, celebratory dances, festive food, decorated dishes, embroidered tablecloths. These manifestations of a vibrant women's culture reflect women's history and current social status. Like everyday language, they are rooted in the material world, yet they are emotionally expressive as well. They are the equivalent of multiracial men's subversive cultural productions, such as jazz and rap, and equally distinctive from the dominant group's way of talking and thinking.

Critique. Some multiracial feminist protests are universal, understood by disadvantaged women everywhere, and some are specific to women's different racial and ethnic groups. African American women, Latinas, and Asian American women may all encounter racial prejudice in social encounters, but they have markedly different experiences in the job market. A question that is difficult to answer is whether the discrimination these women experience is specific to them as women or whether they share racial and ethnic oppression with their men. If racial, ethnic, and gender identity are as intertwined as multiracial feminism claims, then political unity with men of the same racial or ethnic group could severely undermine a consciousness of oppression as women.

Among African Americans, there has been a controversy over whether Black women's independence and assertiveness threaten their men's ego and sense of masculinity. When this view is adopted by White politicians, it becomes an agenda for family policies that make it extremely difficult for battered women to leave abusive men. Where, then, do a woman's loyalty, identification, and politics lie? It may not be with the men of their own racial or ethnic group, who may oppress their own women because of a traditional patriarchal culture or because they themselves are oppressed by men at the top of the pyramid. Men's and women's standpoints within the same group may differ considerably, even though they may share a sense of injustice from their mutual racial or ethnic status.

Politically, however, women of oppressed groups may feel they have to stand by their men. In one Portuguese working-class community in which a woman was repeatedly raped in a pool hall, the women of the town first rallied around her. When the national media came in and began to vilify the men racially, the women turned on the rape victim, accusing her of sexual looseness and child neglect, and supported the men at the trial.

A politics based on identity is a complex of interlocking coalitions and oppositional groups. Consciousness of subordination and the forms of struggle may have to be different for women and men; the man who is Other may need to find the voice suppressed by the dominant men; the woman who is Other may need to find the voice suppressed by both dominant *and* subordinate men.

Summary

Throughout the twentieth century, social critics have argued about which aspect of inequality is the most damaging. Feminists have focused on women's oppression, and civil rights activists on raising the status of the members of a particular disadvantaged racial or ethnic group. Marxist and socialist men and women have been in the forefront of working-class political struggles. Multiracial feminism argues that all these aspects of subordination have to be fought at the same time.

The important point made by multiracial feminism is that a member of a subordinate group is not disadvantaged just by gender or race or ethnicity or social class, but by a *multiple system of domination*. Multiracial feminism is therefore critical of feminist theories that contrast two global groups—"women" and "men." It argues that in racist societies, no one is just a woman or man; they are, in the United States, for example, a White woman or a Black woman, a White man or a Black man.

The combination of social statuses makes for a particular group standpoint—values, sense of appropriate behavior, and outlook on life (which may be completely distinctive or may overlap with that of other groups). The dominant group's standpoint is the one that prevails in the definition of social problems, in the attribution of their causes, and in allocation of resources to research and to political solutions. Members of disadvantaged racial, ethnic, and economic groups have fought to have their points of view heard, as have women. In the political arena, however, sometimes women band with other women and sometimes with men of their own social group. The politics of identity, as multiracial feminism is so aware, is a complex of shifting sides.

Multiracial feminism brings to feminism the tools of racial, ethnic, and class analysis. It gives us a powerful theory of how intersectionality of the multiple social statuses that shape individual lives and organize local communities and nations. Politically, however, multiracial feminism is often caught between the politics of race and ethnicity and that of gender, just as marxist feminists were divided over whether class position is more important than being a woman.

Suggested Readings in Multiracial Feminism

Collins, Patricia Hill. 1990. *Black Feminist Thought: Knowledge, Consciousness, and the Politics of Empowerment.* Boston: Unwin Hyman.

Davis, Angela Y. 1983. *Women, Race and Class.* New York: Vintage.

DuBois, Ellen Carol, and Vicki L. Ruiz (eds.). 1990. *Unequal Sisters: A Multicultural Reader in U.S. Women's History.* New York and London: Routledge.

Glenn, Evelyn Nakano. 1986. *Issei, Nissei, War Bride.* Philadelphia: Temple University Press.

Hooks, Bell. 1984. *Feminist Theory: From Margin to Center.* Boston: South End Press.

—. 1989. *Talking Back: Thinking Feminist, Talking Black.* Boston: South End Press.

—. 1990. *Yearning: Race, Gender, and Cultural Politics.* Boston, MA: South End Press.

Jones, Jacqueline. 1986. *Labor of Love, Labor of Sorrow: Black Women, Work, and the Family from Slavery to the Present.* New York: Vintage.

Melhuus, Marit, and Kristi Anne Stolen (eds.). 1997. *Machos, Mistresses, Madonnas: Contesting the Power of Latin American Gender Imagery.* New York and London: Verso.

Moraga, Cherrie, and Gloria Anzalduá (eds.). 1981. *This Bridge Called My Back: Writings by Radical Women of Color.* Watertown, MA: Persephone Press.

Spivak, Gayatri Chakravorty. 1988. *In Other Worlds: Essays in Cultural Politics.* New York and London: Routledge.

Stack, Carol B. 1975. *All Our Kin: Strategies for Survival in a Black Community.* San Francisco: Harper & Row.

Trinh, T. Minh-ha. 1989. *Woman, Native, Other: Writing Postcoloniality and Feminism.* Bloomington: Indiana University Press.

Walker, Alice. 1984. *In Search of Our Mothers' Gardens: Womanist Prose.* New York: Harcourt Brace.

Wallace, Michele. [1978] 1990. *Black Macho and the Myth of the Superwoman.* London: Verso.

Chapter Nine

Men's Feminism

Sources of Gender Inequality

- Dominance of economic and educational resources and political power by one group of men
- Institutionalized privileges that benefit all men
- Social values that encourage men's violence and sexual exploitation of women

Remedies

- Share resources and power
- Enhance women's status and also that of disadvantaged men, including homosexuals
- Make men responsible for controlling their own violent behavior

Contributions

- Analysis of men's gender as part of a set of institutionalized relationships of dominance and subordination
- Recognition of men's dominance of other men as well as of women
- Critique of the culture of violence in sports

M en's feminism applies feminist theories to the study of men and masculinity. Men's feminism took on the task called for by feminists studying women in relationship to men—to treat men as well as women as a gender and to scrutinize masculinity as carefully as femininity. A prime goal has been to develop a theory, not of masculinity but of masculinities, because of the diversity among men. Men's feminism argues that although a pattern of social dominance over women is prevalent, there are no universal masculine characteristics that are the same in every society—nor, for that matter, within any one society, or in any one organizational setting, as earlier studies of working-class men, Black men, and men under colonial domination made very clear.

The main theory developed in men's feminism, which has been used to dissect the differences between and within groups of upper-, middle-, and working-class men of different ethnic groups and sexual orientations in Western society, is a concept of *hegemonic masculinity*. Men who have the most valued characteristics in Western society—who are economically successful, from racially and ethnically privileged groups, and visibly heterosexual—are at the top of the social ladder. They may be of poor or working-class origins, but most have been educated at good colleges and universities and have professional or managerial careers. Their dominant status is justified by these valued or hegemonic attributes. They are both born to these characteristics (e.g., whiteness) and achieve them (education). But what they can achieve depends partly on what they are born to.

Yet the characteristics of masculinity, hegemonic or otherwise, are not the source of men's gender status. Genders—men's and women's—are relational and embedded in the structure of the social order. The object of analysis in men's feminism is thus not masculinity alone but its oppositional relationship to femininity. Much of masculinity is non-femininity (and vice versa). Neither men nor woman can be studied separately; the whole question of gender inequality involves all men's supposed superiority to women and some men's supposed superiority to other men.

The following excerpt about the subject under scrutiny—masculinity—is by Bob Connell, an Australian social scientist who is one of the main theorists of men's feminism. He argues that the physiological markers of maleness cannot identify masculine characteristics or men's status because the meanings of masculinity vary historically, culturally, and geographically. As for status, a man's position in the gendered social order is understandable only in relation to women and other men.

Studying Masculinity

R. W. Connell

Once we recognize the institutional dimension of gender it is difficult to avoid the question: is it actually masculinity that is a gender politics? Or is it rather the institutional arrangements that produce inequality, and thus generate the tensions that have brought 'masculinity' under scrutiny?

It is certainly important to acknowledge a social dynamic in its own right, and not try to read it off from men's psychology. Yet it is difficult to deny gay men's experiences of the personal emotion in homophobia, women's experiences of misogyny, or feminist arguments about the importance of desire and motive in the reproduction of patriarchy. Whatever is significant in issues about masculinity involves both personality and social relations; centrally it involves the interplay between the two.

But is there a stable object of knowledge in this interplay? Can there be literally a science of masculinity? . . .

There is no masculine entity whose occurrences in all societies we can generalize about. The things designated by the term in different cases are logically incommensurable.

Positivism has one line of escape from this difficulty. What is more or less constant, through the shifts of culture, is the anatomy and physiology of male bodies. We could pursue a science of *men*, defining 'masculinity' as the character of anyone who possessed a penis, a Y chromosome and a certain supply of testosterone. A recent French book about masculinity, one of the better popular books about men, is simply called *XY*. This is, perhaps, what is ultimately implied by the idea of 'men's studies.'

This solves the logical problem, but it is not likely to lead to a science worth having. It is unmanageably vague: what action of any man in the world would *not* be an instance of masculinity? It would be impossible in such a framework to explore one of the main issues raised by psychoanalysis, the masculinity within women and the femininity within men. To believe that we can understand the social world through a biological demarcation is to misunderstand the relation between bodies and social processes. . . .

Masculinity and femininity are inherently relational concepts, which have meaning in relation to each other, as a social demarcation and a cultural opposition. This holds regardless of the changing content of the demarcation in different societies and periods of history. Masculinity as an object of knowledge is always masculinity-in-relation.

To put the point in another and perhaps clearer way, it is *gender relations* that constitute a coherent object of knowledge for science. Knowledge of masculinity arises within the project of knowing gender relations. . . . Masculinities are configurations of practice structured by gender relations. They are inherently historical; and their making and remaking is a political process affecting the balance of interests in society and the direction of social change.

We can have systematic knowledge of such objects, but this knowledge does not follow the model of positivist science. Studies of a historical, political reality must work with the category of possibility. They grasp the world that is brought into being through social action in the light of the possibilities not realized, as well as those that are realized. Such knowledge is based on a critique of the real, not just a reflection of it.

Critical social science requires an ethical baseline empirically grounded in the situations under study. The baseline for the analysis in this book is social justice: the objective possibility of justice in gender relations, a possibility sometimes realized and sometimes not. To adopt such a baseline is not to propose an arbitrary value preference that is separate from the act of knowing. Rather, it is to acknowledge the inherently political character of our knowledge of masculinity. We can treat that as an epistemological asset, not an embarrassment.

In this sense we can have a meaningful science of masculinity. It is part of the critical science of gender relations and their trajectory in history. That, in turn, is part of the larger exploration of human possibility, and its negations, which both social science and practical politics require.

Men's feminism argues that gender inequality includes men's denigration of other men as well as their exploitation of women. Low-level men workers around the world are oppressed by the inequalities of the global economy, and young working-class urban men's impoverished environment and "taste for risk" has made them an endangered species. Men's feminism blames sports, the military, fraternities, and other arenas of male bonding for encouraging physical and sexual violence and misogyny. It deplores the social pressure on men to identify with but not be emotionally close to their fathers and to be "cool" and unfeeling towards the women in their lives and distant from their own children.

While men's feminism uses psychoanalytic theories of the need to detach from the mother to explain men's emotional repression, it is critical of men's movements that foster a search for the inner primitive, or "wild man." It also regards religiously oriented men's organizations, such as Promise Keepers, as dangerous to women's autonomy because they link responsibility to family with patriarchal concepts of manhood. Men's feminism argues that these movements seek to change individual attitudes and do not address the structural conditions of gender inequality or the power differences between men and women and among men.

The gender politics that men's feminism concentrates on is embedded in the stratification systems of Western societies— racial and economic—as well as in the masculine dread of homosexuals. Prominent men of all racial and ethnic groups in politics, sports, and the mass media must appear heterosexual, which sometimes leads to constant womanizing. Men's feminism also criticizes the jockeying for leading positions in whatever arena men find themselves. It is not an accident that so much of the language of competition is the language of sports, because organized sports not only are an immediate site for demonstrations of masculinity but are also a source for vicarious competitiveness and for the creation of icons of masculine strength and beauty. Unfortunately, many athletes who have attained icon status are prone to use physical and sexual violence.

Men's feminism says that office-bound men's identification with the bruisers on the football field allows them to feel masculine and yet above such gross displays of physicality. White middle-class men who participate vicariously in the violent professional sports played by mostly Black and Hispanic men from economically disadvantaged backgrounds (but now very rich) admire their masculine physical prowess, extravagant wealth, and flaunted sexuality, but they also maintain their own racial and class superiority. White middle-class men who are themselves involved in professional sports are most of the owners, lawyers, agents, financial managers, journalists, and advertisers who make the athletes' careers. As a significant source of the social construction of masculinities in Western society, sport stratifies men, as can be seen from the following excerpt by the 1995 president of the North American Society for the Sociology of Sport.

WATCHING MEN'S SPORT, CONSTRUCTING MASCULINITIES

Michael A. Messner

What does televised sport mean to male viewers? The mythology and symbolism of today's most popular spectator sports are probably meaningful to viewers on a number of levels: patriotism, militarism, violence, and meritocracy are all dominant themes. But it is reasonable to speculate that gender is a salient organizing theme in the construction of meanings, especially with respect to the more aggressive and violent aspects of sport. For example, when I was interviewing a thirty-two-year-old white professional-class male, and I asked him how he felt about the fact that recently a woman had been promoted to a position of authority in his workplace, he replied, "A woman can do the same job as I can do—maybe even be my boss. But I'll be *damned* if she can go out on the [football] field and take a hit from Ronnie Lott."

At the most obvious level, we can read this man's statement as an indication that he is identifying with Ronnie Lott as a man, and the basis of the identification is the violent male body. Football, based as it is on the fullest potential of the male body (muscular bulk, explosive power) is clearly a world apart from women, who are relegated to the roles of sex objects on the sidelines, rooting their men on. In contrast to the bare and vulnerable bodies of the cheerleaders, the armored male bodies of the football players are elevated to mythical status and thus give testimony to the undeniable "fact" that here is at least one place where men are clearly superior to women. Yet it is also significant that this man was quite aware that he (and perhaps 99 percent of the rest of the male population of the United States) was probably equally incapable of taking a "hit" from the likes of Ronnie Lott and living to tell of it. I would speculate that by recognizing the simultaneous construction of identification and difference among men, we may begin to understand the major role that televised sport plays in the current gender order.

Identification. With the twentieth-century decline of the practical relevance of physical strength in work and in warfare, representations of the male body as strong, virile, and powerful have taken on increasingly important ideological and symbolic significance in gender relations. Indeed, the body plays such a central role in the contemporary gender order because it is so closely associated with the "natural." Yet, as we have seen, though the body is popularly equated with nature, it is nevertheless an object of social practice: The development of men's bodies for athletic competition takes a tremendous amount of time, exercise, weight-training, and even use of illegal and dangerous drugs such as steroids. But the sport media tend to obscure the reality of this social construction, weaving a cloak of symbol and interpretation around these gendered bodies that naturalizes them.

Some recent theorists have suggested that the true significance of sport as mediated spectacle lies in male spectators having the opportunity to identify narcissistically with the muscular male body. . . . Rather than concluding that televised sport violence has no meaning, it is reasonable to speculate that if men are using sport spectatorship to identify with the male body as a thing of beauty and power, perhaps the violence is an important aspect of the denial of the homoerotic element of that identification.

Difference. It is also possible that the media's framing of sport violence plays another important role: the construction of difference among men. As we have seen, it is disproportionately males from lower socioeconomic and ethnic minority backgrounds who commit themselves to athletic careers, and who end up participating at the higher levels of aggressive, violent sports. Privileged men might, as Woody Guthrie once suggested, commit violence against others "with fountain pens," but with the exception of domestic violence against women and children, physical violence is rarely a part of the everyday lives of these men. Yet violence among men may still have important ideological and psychological meaning for men from privileged backgrounds. There is a curious preoccupation among middle-class males with movie characters who are "working-class tough guys," with athletes who are fearsome "hitters" and who heroically "play hurt." These violent "tough guys" of the culture industry—the Rambos, the Ronnie Lotts—are at once the heroes who "prove" that "we men" are superior to women and the "other" against whom privileged men define themselves as "modern.". . .

Men's feminism overlaps with gay studies in analyzing the social dimensions of male homosexuality. Examining homosexuality from a gender perspective shows that homosexual men are *men*, not a third gender, and partake of the privileges (or lack of them) and life style of men of the same ethnic group and social class. Nonetheless, because homosexual men do not have sexual relationships with women—an important marker of manhood in Western society—they are considered not-quite-men. Thus, like other men who do not have the marks of dominant status (being White, economically successful, heterosexual), homosexual men are lower on the scale of privilege and power in Western society. Homosexual men, however, do not subvert the gender order because they retain some of the "patriarchal dividend" of men's status.

Critique. Men's feminism provides a needed corrective in bringing men into gender research as a specific subject of study, but it does not offer a new theoretical perspective. Rather, men's feminism is an amalgam of psychoanalytic, multiracial, social construction, and gay studies. Women feminists have also written about masculinity, men's roles at work and in the family, and how men are changing—but slowly. The question, then, is whether men's feminism brings a different view on men's status because men themselves are writing about it.

Feminist men's politics include trying to educate young men about date rape and fraternity gang rape. Others who were athletes have written and lectured about the violent values in sport. Black and Hispanic men feminists have analyzed the dangers of risk taking and machismo. Gay men have analyzed and documented the history of the social construction of homosexuality, and its recent path from the headiness of the Greenwich Village Stonewall riot to the tragedies of AIDS. There is a comprehensive body of knowledge in men's feminism, but politically, the men's movement has been taken over by the Iron Johns and the Promise Keepers, who offer versions of masculinity that are not much different from the conventional beliefs in men's intrinsic "wildness" or need to be the "head of the house."

Another strand in the nonfeminist politics of masculinity is the argument that says that men's power is a myth because so many men's roles are dangerous. They, and not women, are exploited—fighting wars, fires, criminals, and terrorists. Women feminists, not men, have countered this argument with studies of women in the military, the police, and other occupations where formerly only men showed they had the "right stuff." (Women could not enter such occupations until fairly recently.) A woman feminist has documented men's rapid rise up the "glass escalator" to the top positions in *women's* occupations. Both types of data—that women can do the dangerous work men do and that men doing women's work have the advantage of their dominant gender status—are analyses that came from women's, not men's, feminism.

If men's feminism is to add the dimension of the insider's view, they have to turn the gender lens on themselves in all the areas where men still dominate—fundamentalist religions, science, politics, the higher echelons of finance, and the capitalist markets of the global economy.

Summary

Men's feminism has brought attention to the fact that men as well as women have a gender status. Men's gender status is dominant in most societies, although there is a hierarchy of dominant and subordinate men. Even though disadvantaged men may be lower on the status scale than dominant men, they are usually dominant over the women of their own group. The analysis of the structure of privilege, as well as the sexist practices and violent behavior that maintain men's dominance, have been dissected and deplored by men's feminism.

In particular, men's feminism has shown that the racial and economic stratification in sports and its culture of violence takes a high toll on the players and on aspiring teenagers. A few professional athletes have careers that are rewarding financially and in popularity, but for the most part, the money in sport is made by White, middle-class men. In the health field, the high death rate of young men from poor urban centers and the short life expectancy of older men have been attributed to gendered, racial, ethnic, and economic pressures.

Men's feminism should be distinguished from the men's movements that focus on individual change. From the point of view of men's feminism, bonding with symbolic brothers and fathers and dancing to drums in a wood may make men more emotionally expressive, but it does nothing about the structural sources of gender inequality. Men's feminism also criticizes movements that offer men a rightful place as heads of their families in exchange for the promise of taking responsibility for the welfare of their wives and children. Men's feminism would rather see men and women sharing family work and economic support as equal partners. Men's feminism has also undertaken an active program of anti-rape and anti-battering education.

Men's feminism uses many of the ideas of women's feminism. It is currently a parallel field of study focusing on men and masculinity, but with overlaps in research on the body, sexuality, violence, personality development, health, and family relationships.

Suggested Readings in Men's Feminism

Brod, Harry, and Michael Kaufman (eds.). 1994. *Theorizing Masculinities*. Newbury Park, CA: Sage.

Connell, R. W. 1995. *Masculinities*. Berkeley: University of California Press.

Hearn, Jeff, and David Morgan (eds.). 1990. *Men, Masculinities and Social Theory*. London: Unwin Hyman.

Kimmel, Michael S. (ed.). 1991. *Men Confront Pornography*. New York: Meridian.

——. 1996. *Manhood in America: A Cultural History*. New York: Free Press.

Majors, Richard, and Janet Mancini Billson. 1992. *Cool Pose: The Dilemmas of Black Manhood in America*. New York: Lexington Books.

Messner, Michael A. 1992. *Power at Play: Sports and the Problem of Masculinity*. Boston: Beacon Press.

——. 1997. *Politics of Masculinities: Men in Movements*. Newbury Park, CA: Sage.

Messner, Michael A., and Donald F. Sabo (eds.). 1990. *Sport, Men, and the Gender Order: Critical Feminist Perspectives*. Champaign, IL: Human Kinetics.

Sabo, Don, and David Frederick Gordon (eds.). 1995. *Men's Health and Illness: Gender, Power and the Body*. Newbury Park, CA: Sage.

Schwalbe, Michael. 1996. *Unlocking the Iron Cage: The Men's Movement, Gender Politics, and American Culture*. New York: Oxford University Press.

Staples, Robert. 1982. *Black Masculinity: The Black Male's Roles in American Society*. San Francisco, CA: Black Scholar Press.

Stoltenberg, John. 1990. *Refusing to Be a Man: Essays on Sex and Justice*. New York: Meridian.

Williams, Christine L. 1995. *Still a Man's World: Men Who Do Women's Work*. Berkeley: University of California Press.

Chapter Ten

Social Construction Feminism

Sources of Gender Inequality

- Social construction of gender differences and constant re-creation of the boundaries between gender categories
- Work and family based on two and only two genders
- Women as an exploitable category in the gendered social order

Remedies

- Make the processes of gender construction visible
- Challenge gender boundaries in everyday life
- Restructure work and family roles so they are not based on a gendered division of labor

Contributions

- A theory of gender that connects face-to-face interaction with institutional structures
- Analysis of the social construction of sexuality and its social control

- Refutation of the biological underpinnings of gender by showing how science constructs sex categories

While multiracial feminism focuses on how women suffer from the effects of a system of racial and ethnic disadvantage, and men's feminism focuses on the hierarchical relationships of men to other men and to women, social construction feminism looks at the structure of the gendered social order as a whole and at the processes that construct and maintain it. Social construction feminism sees gender as a society-wide institution that is built into all the major social organizations of society. As a social institution, gender determines the distribution of power, privileges, and economic resources. Through parenting, the schools, and the mass media, gendered norms and expectations get built into boys' and girls' sense of self as a certain kind of human being. By the time people get to be adults, alternative ways of acting and arranging work and family life are literally unthinkable.

Although teachers today are attuned to the dangers of treating boys and girls differently, they still separate them in class teams and do not encourage their playing together in games or sports. Children who behave in gender-appropriate ways are considered normal; anything else (girls insulting, threatening, and physically fighting boys and other girls; boys who do not like sports and who cry a lot) is considered "gender deviance."

The family is another prime site for the social construction of gender differences. In dual-earner families, women do more housework than the men they live with even if they work longer hours and make more money. In most households, women do most of the daily cooking, cleaning, and laundry. Men's jobs around the house are usually outdoor work, repairs, and car maintenance. Keeping your house neat, dressing your children in clean clothes, and feeding your family means you are a good woman. Work for the family not only maintains the household, it also reinforces gender.

Similarly, whether the husband or the wife is the main economic support of the household, the husband is considered the breadwinner and the wife the "extra" earner. A good man supports his family. His income is allocated to what are considered the necessities—paying the rent or mortgage, paying electric and heating bills, making car payments, buying basic furniture and the groceries. The wife's income goes to the extras the family often cannot do without—school fees, clothing, bed linens and window curtains—as well as the supposed luxuries like vacations and babysitters. The gendered division of financial responsibility for the family fits neatly into the gendered salary scales in the job market—bosses can justify paying women less because everyone considers a married woman's husband to be the breadwinner. Women who are the sole support of their household and married men who are poor earners particularly suffer from these inequities.

The social construction of gender not only produces the differences between men's and women's characteristics and behavior, it also produces gender inequality. Yet we cannot stop "doing gender" because it is part of our basic identity. In a social order based on gender divisions, everyone always "does gender" almost all the time. The following excerpt, from an article that has become a classic of social construction feminism, lays out the interconnections between "doing gender" in the course of everyday life and the build-up of both gendered self-identity and gendered social structures.

Doing Gender

Candace West and Don H. Zimmerman

. . . Our purpose in this article is to propose an ethnomethodologically informed, and therefore distinctively sociological, understanding of gender as a routine, methodical, and recurring accomplishment. We contend that the "doing" of gender is undertaken by women and men whose competence as members of society is hostage to its production. Doing gender involves a complex of socially guided perceptual, interactional, and micropolitical activities that cast particular pursuits as expressions of masculine and feminine "natures."

When we view gender as an accomplishment, an achieved property of situated conduct, our attention shifts from matters internal to the individual and focuses on interactional and, ultimately, institutional arenas. In one sense, of course, it is individuals who "do" gender. But it is a situated doing, carried out in the virtual or real presence of others who are presumed to be oriented to its production. Rather than as a property of individuals, we conceive of gender as an emergent feature of social situations: both as an outcome of and a rationale for various social arrangements and as a means of legitimating one of the most fundamental divisions of society.

To advance our argument, we undertake a critical examination of what sociologists have meant by *gender*, including its treatment as a role enactment in the conventional sense and as a "display" in Goffman's (1976) terminology. Both *gender role* and *gender display* focus on behavioral aspects of being a woman or a man (as opposed, for example, to biological differences between the two). However, we contend that the notion of gender as a role obscures the work that is involved in producing gender in everyday activities, while the notion of gender as a display relegates it to the periphery of interaction. We argue instead that participants in interaction organize their various and manifold activities to reflect or express gender, and they are disposed to perceive the behavior of others in a similar light.

To elaborate our proposal, we suggest at the outset that important but often overlooked distinctions be observed among *sex, sex category*, and *gender*. *Sex* is a determination made through the application of socially agreed upon biological criteria for classifying persons as females or males. The criteria for classification can be genitalia at birth or chromosomal typing before birth, and they do not necessarily agree with one another. Placement in a *sex category* is achieved through application of the sex criteria, but in everyday life, categorization is established and sustained by the socially required identificatory displays that proclaim one's membership in one or the other category. In this sense, one's sex category presumes one's sex and stands as proxy for it in many situations, but sex and sex category can vary independently; that is, it is possible to claim membership in a sex category even when the sex criteria are lacking. *Gender*, in contrast, is the activity of managing situated conduct in light of normative conceptions of attitudes and activities appropriate for one's sex category. Gender activities emerge from and bolster claims to membership in a sex category.

We contend that recognition of the analytical independence of sex, sex category, and gender is essential for understanding the relationships among these elements and the interactional work involved in "being" a gendered person in society. . . .

Garfinkel's (1967, pp. 118–40) case study of Agnes, a transsexual raised as a boy who adopted a female identity at age 17 and underwent a sex reassignment operation several years later, demonstrates how gender is created through interaction and at the same time structures interaction. Agnes, whom Garfinkel characterized as a "practical methodologist," developed a number of procedures for passing as a "normal, natural female" both prior to and after her surgery. She had the practical task of managing the fact that she possessed male genitalia and that she lacked the social resources a girl's biography would presumably provide in everyday interaction. In short, she needed to display herself as a woman, simultaneously learning what it was to be a woman. Of necessity, this full-time pursuit took place at a time when most people's gender would be well-accredited and routinized. Agnes had to consciously contrive what the vast majority of women do without thinking. She was not "faking" what "real" women do naturally. She was obliged to analyze and figure out how to act within socially structured circumstances and conceptions of femininity that women born with appropriate biological credentials come to take for granted early on. As in the case of others who must "pass," such as transvestites, Kabuki actors, or Dustin Hoffman's "Tootsie," Agnes's case makes visible what culture has made invisible—the accomplishment of gender. . . .

Doing gender means creating differences between girls and boys and women and men, differences that are not natural, essential, or biological. Once the differences have been constructed, they are used to reinforce the "essentialness"of gender. In a delightful account of the "arrangement between the sexes," Goffman (1977) observes the creation of a variety of institutionalized frameworks through which our "natural, normal sexedness" can be enacted. The physical features of social setting provide one obvious resource for the expression of our "essential" differences. For example, the sex segregation of North American public bathrooms distinguishes "ladies" from "gentlemen" in matters held to be fundamentally biological, even though both "are somewhat similar in the question of waste products and their elimination" (Goffman 1977, p. 315). These settings are furnished with dimorphic equipment (such as urinals for men or elaborate grooming facilities for women), even though both sexes may achieve the same ends through the same means (and apparently do so in the privacy of their own homes). . . .

Can we avoid doing gender? Earlier, we proposed that insofar as sex category is used as a fundamental criterion for differentiation, doing gender is unavoidable. It is unavoidable because of the social consequences of sex-category membership: the allocation of power and resources not only in the domestic, economic, and political domains but also in the broad arena of interpersonal relations. In virtually any situation, one's sex category can be relevant, and one's performance as an incumbent of that category (i.e., gender) can be subjected to evaluation. Maintaining such pervasive and faithful assignment of lifetime status requires legitimation.

But doing gender also renders the social arrangements based on sex category accountable as normal and natural, that is, legitimate ways of organizing social life. Differences between women and men that are created by this process can then be portrayed as fundamental and enduring dispositions. In this light, the institutional arrangements of a society can be seen as responsive to the differences—the social order being merely an accommodation to the natural order. Thus if, in doing gender, men are also doing dominance and women are doing deference (cf. Goffman 1967, pp. 47–95), the resultant social order, which supposedly reflects "natural differences," is a powerful reinforcer and legitimator of hierarchical arrangements. Frye observes:

> For efficient subordination, what's wanted is that the structure not appear to be a cultural artifact kept in place by human decision or custom, but that it appear *natural*—that it appear to be quite a direct consequence of facts about the beast which are beyond the scope of human manipulation. . . . That we are trained to behave so differently as women and men, and to behave so differently toward women and men, itself contributes mightily to the appearance of extreme dimorphism, but also, the *ways* we act as women and men, and the ways we act toward women and men, mold our bodies and our minds to the shape of subordination and dominance. We do become what we practice being. (Frye 1983, p. 34)

If we do gender appropriately, we simultaneously sustain, reproduce, and render legitimate the institutional arrangements that are based on sex category. If we fail to do gender appropriately, we as individuals—not the institutional arrangements—may be called to account (for our character, motives, and predispositions).

Social movements such as feminism can provide the ideology and impetus to question existing arrangements, and the social support for individuals to explore alternatives to them. Legislative changes, such as that proposed by the Equal Rights Amendment, can also weaken the accountability of conduct to sex category, thereby affording the possibility of more widespread loosening of accountability in general. To be sure, equality under the law does not guarantee equality in other arenas. As Lorber (1986, p. 577) points out, assurance of "scrupulous equality of categories of people considered essentially different needs constant monitoring." What such proposed changes *can* do is provide the warrant for asking why, if we wish to treat women and men as equals, there needs to be two sex categories at all (see Lorber 1986, p. 577).

The sex category/gender relationship links the institutional and interactional levels, a coupling that legitimates social arrangements based on sex category and reproduces their asymmetry in face-to-face interaction. Doing gender furnishes the interactional scaffolding of social structure, along with a built-in mechanism of social control. In appreciating the institutional forces that maintain distinctions between women and men, we must not lose sight of the interactional validation of those distinctions that confers upon them their sense of "naturalness" and "rightness."

Social change, then, must be pursued both at the institutional and cultural level of sex category and at the interactional level of gender. Such a conclusion is hardly novel. Nevertheless, we suggest that it is important to recognize that the analytical distinction between institutional and interactional spheres does not pose an either/or choice when it comes to the question of effecting social change. Reconceptualizing gender not as a simple property of individuals but as an integral dynamic of social orders implies a new perspective on the entire network of gender relations:

> [t]he social subordination of women, and the cultural practices which help sustain it; the politics of sexual object-choice, and particularly the oppression of homosexual people; the sexual division of labor, the formation of character and motive, so far as they are organized as femininity and masculinity; the role of the body in social relations, especially the politics of childbirth; and the nature of strategies of sexual liberation movements. (Connell 1985, p. 261)

Gender is a powerful ideological device, which produces, reproduces, and legitimates the choices and limits that are predicated on sex category. An understanding of how gender is produced in social situations will afford clarification of the interactional scaffolding of social structure and the social control processes that sustain it.

References

Connell, R. W. 1985. "Theorizing Gender." *Sociology* 19:260–72.

Frye, Marilyn. 1983. *The Politics of Reality: Essays in Feminist Theory.* Trumansburg, NY: The Crossing Press.

Garfinkel, Harold. 1967. *Studies in Ethnomethodology.* Englewood Cliffs, NJ: Prentice-Hall.

Goffman, Erving. [1956] 1967. "The Nature of Deference and Demeanor." Pp. 47–95 in *Interaction Ritual.* New York: Anchor/Doubleday.

——. 1976. "Gender Display." *Studies in the Anthropology of Visual Communication.* 3:69–77.

——. 1977. "The Arrangement Between the Sexes." *Theory and Society* 4:301–31.

Lorber, Judith. 1986. "Dismantling Noah's Ark." *Sex Roles* 14:567-80.

In social construction feminist theory, inequality is the core of gender itself: Women and men are socially differentiated in order to justify treating them unequally. Thus, although gender is intertwined with other unequal statuses, remedying the gendered part of these structures of inequality may be the most difficult, because gendering is so pervasive. Indeed, it is this pervasiveness that leads so many people to believe that gendering is biological, and therefore "natural."

Politically, social construction feminism wants the same degendering of work, family, and other roles that liberal feminism argues for. But their theories differ—liberal feminism claims that women and men are very similar in their behavior despite their biological differences. Social construction feminism goes further, arguing that the dichotomies of male and female biological sex and physiology are also produced and maintained by social processes. Genital and hormonal ambiguities are ignored or overridden in the sex categorization of infants, and the gendering of sports and physical labor ignores the overlaps in female and male stature and musculature. This theoretical point is significant, because so many of our beliefs about what women and men can and should do derive their power from assumptions about biological input. Social construction feminism uses standpoint feminism's critique of science to bolster its politics of gender blurring.

Sexuality, too, is socially constructed. The following excerpt from Thomas Laqueur's history of the social construction of gendered sexual bodies in Western culture shows how and why Freud moved female orgasms from the clitoris to the vagina.

Clitoral and Vaginal Orgasms

Thomas Laqueur

Like a Bahktiari tribesman in search of fresh pastures, female sexuality is said to migrate from one place to another, from the malelike clitoris to the unmistakably female vagina. The clitoris does not, however, entirely lose its function as a result of pleasure's short but significant journey. Instead it becomes the organ *through which* excitement is transmitted to the "adjacent female sexual parts," to its permanent home, the true locus of a woman's erotic life, the vagina. The clitoris, in Freud's less than illuminating simile, becomes "like pine shavings" used "to set a log of harder wood on fire."

This strangely inappropriate identification of the cavity of the vagina with a burning log is not my concern here. Stranger still is what happens to biology in Freud's famous essay. A little girl's realization that she does not have a penis and that therefore her sexuality resides in its supposed opposite, in the cavity of the vagina, elevates a "biological fact" into a cultural desideratum. Freud writes as if he has discovered the basis in anatomy for the entire nineteenth-century world of gender. In an age obsessed with being able to justify and distinguish the social roles of women and men, science seems to have found in the radical difference of penis and vagina not just a sign of sexual difference but its very foundation. When erotogenic susceptibility to stimulation has been successfully transferred by a woman from the clitoris to the vaginal orifice, she has adopted a new leading zone for the purposes of her later sexual activity.

Freud goes even further by suggesting that the repression of female sexuality in puberty, marked by abandonment of the clitoris, heightens male desire and thus tightens the web of heterosexual union on which reproduction, the family, and indeed civilization itself appear to rest: "The intensification of the brake upon sexuality brought about by pubertal repression in women serves as a stimulus to the libido of men and causes an increase in its activity." (Freud [1905] 1962, 124) When everything has settled down, the "masculine machinery" of the clitoris is abandoned, the vagina is erotically charged, and the body is set for reproductive intercourse. Freud seems to be taking a stab at historical bio-anthropology, claiming that female modesty incites male desire while female acquiescence, in allowing it to be gratified, leads humanity out of the savage's cave.

Perhaps this is pushing one paragraph too hard, but Freud in these passages is very much in the imaginative footsteps of Diderot and Rousseau, who argued that civilization began when women began to discriminate, to limit her availability. Freud in the *Three Essays* is not quite so explicit, but he does appear to be arguing that femininity, and thus the place of women in society, is grounded in the developmental neurology of the female genitals.

But could he really have meant this? In the first place, the long written history of the body would have shown that the vagina fails miserably as a "natural symbol" of interior sexuality, of passivity, of the private against the public, of a critical stage in the ontogeny of woman. In the one-sex model, dominant in anatomical thinking for two thousand years, woman was understood as man inverted: the uterus was the female scrotum, the ovaries were testicles, the vulva was a foreskin, and *the vagina was a penis*. This account of sexual difference, though as phallocentric as Freud's, offered no real female interior, only the displacement inward to a more sheltered space of the male organs, as if the scrotum and penis in the form of uterus and vagina had taken cover from the cold.

If Freud was not aware of this history, he surely must have known that there was absolutely no anatomical or physiological evidence for the claim that "erotogenic susceptibility to stimulation" is successfully transferred during the maturation of women "from the clitoris to the vaginal orifice." The abundance of specialized nerve endings in the clitoris and the relative impoverishment of the vagina had been demonstrated half a century before Freud wrote and had been known in outline for hundreds of years. Common medical knowledge available in any nineteenth-century handbook thus makes Freud's story a puzzle, if it is construed as a narrative of biology. Finally, if the advent of the vaginal orgasm were the consequence of neurological processes, then Freud's question of "how a woman develops out of a child with bisexual dispositions" could be resolved by physiology without any help from psychoanalysis.

Freud's answer, then, must be regarded as a narrative of culture in anatomical disguise. The tale of the clitoris is a parable of culture, of how the body is forged into a shape valuable to civilization despite, not because of itself. The language of biology gives this tale its rhetorical authority but does not describe a deeper reality in nerves and flesh.

Freud, in short, must have known that he was inventing vaginal orgasm and that he was at the same time giving a radical new meaning to the clitoris. . . . [He] must have known that what he wrote in the language of biology regarding the shift of erotogenic sensibility from the clitoris to the vagina had no basis in the facts of anatomy or physiology. Both the migration of female sexuality and the opposition between the vagina and penis must therefore be understood as re-presentations of a social ideal in yet another form. On a formal level, the opposition of the vagina and penis represents an ideal of parity. The social thuggery that takes a polymorphously perverse infant and bullies it into a heterosexual man or woman finds an organic correlative in the body, in the opposition of the sexes and their organs. Perhaps because Freud is the great theorist of sexual ambiguity, he is also the inventor of a dramatic sexual antithesis: between the embarrassing clitoris that girls desert and the vagina whose erotogenic powers they embrace as mature women.

More generally, what might loosely be called patriarchy may have appeared to Freud as the only possible way to organize the relations between the sexes, leading him to write as if its signs in the body, external active penis versus internal passive vagina, were "natural." But in Freud's question of how it is that "a woman develops out of a child with a bisexual disposition," the word "woman" clearly refers not to natural sex but to theatrical gender, to socially defined roles.

Reference

Freud, Sigmund. [1905] 1962. *Three Essays on the Theory of Sexuality.* (Trans. James Strachey). New York: Avon.

Social construction feminism not only analyzes the historical and cultural context in which sexuality is "scripted," it focuses politically on what sexual behaviors are approved, tolerated, and tabooed for women and men of different social groups. Sexuality, in this perspective, is a product of learning, social pressures, and cultural values. Legal penalties, job loss, and violence uphold the heterosexual social order, defeating individual attempts at resistance and rebellion.

In the social construction perspective, the reaction to deviations from established norms of gender and sexuality are manifestations of power and social control. Religion, the law, and medicine reinforce the boundary lines between women and men and homosexuals and heterosexuals. Sexual and gender rebellion is made sinful, illegal, or insane. However, most people voluntarily go along with their society's prescriptions because the norms and expectations get built into their individual sense of worth and identity. Even transvestites (males who dress in women's clothes and females who dress in men's clothes) and transsexuals (people who have sex-change surgery) try to pass as "normal" men and women. Male cross-dressers tend to wear very feminine-looking clothing, and male transsexuals use hormones to grow breasts. Because contemporary Western men's clothing is acceptable for women to wear, female gender rebels have an easier time "passing."

The power of social construction is evident not only in the re-gendering of the bodies and dress of "transgenders," but in what happens to them in work and family roles. Male-to-female transsexuals find that the jobs they are hired for as women pay less than those they had as men. Transsexuals who are married have to get divorced, because, in our society, two women and two men cannot be legally married. (They can in other societies, as, for example, certain Native American tribes and African societies.) All of a transsexual's identity papers, from birth certificates to passports, have to be reissued in their new gender and name. Changing gender is changing one's basic social status.

In the social construction feminist view, long-lasting change of this deeply gendered social order would have to mean a conscious reordering of the gendered division of labor in the family and at work, and at the same time, undermining the assumptions about the capabilities of women and men that justify the status quo. Such change is unlikely to come about unless the pervasiveness of the social institution of gender and its social construction are openly challenged. Since the processes of gendering end up making them invisible, where are we to start? With individual awareness and attitude change, or with restructuring social institutions and behavioral change? Certainly, both individuals and institutions need to be altered to achieve gender equality, but it may be impossible to do both at once.

Critique. Social construction feminism is faced with a political dilemma. Getting people to understand the constrictions of gender norms and expectations and encouraging resistance to them in daily life will not necessarily change social structures. Couples who have set up egalitarian households and who scrupulously share parenting run into work scheduling problems. Men are still supposed to put work before family, and women, family before work. Conversely, getting work organizations to hire men for women's jobs and women for men's jobs has not changed gender norms. Women bosses are criticized for being too assertive, while men teachers, social workers, and nurses are quickly pushed ahead into administration.

The dilemma of structure and action is built into the theory of social construction. Socially patterned individual actions and institutional structures construct and reinforce each other. People constantly re-create and maintain the gender norms and expectations and patterns of behavior that are built into work and family structures. They may resist or rebel, but the gendered social order is very slow to change.

Summary

Social construction feminism focuses on the processes that both create gender differences and also render the construction of gender invisible. The common social processes that encourage us to see gender differences and to ignore continuums are the gendered division of labor in the home that allocates child care and housework to women; the consensus that only the man is the breadwinner of a family; gender segregation and gender typing of occupations so that women and men do not do the same kind of work; regendering (as when an occupation goes from men's work to women's work and is justified both ways by "natural" masculine and feminine characteristics); selective comparisons that ignore similarities; and containment, suppression, and erasure of gender-inappropriate behaviors and appearances.

Sexuality is also socially constructed. Deviations from what is considered normal for boys and girls are subject to disapproval and punishment by parents, teachers, and peers. In adults, overt sexual deviance, such as homosexuality, is controlled by laws, religions, and psychiatry.

For the most part, people act in approved-of ways because the whole gendered social order is set up for men and women to feel different and act differently. Even when social institutions change, as when girls are admitted to an all-boys' school or men are hired for a "woman's" job such as nurse, gender boundaries are not erased. Ways are found for the girls to be distinguishable from the boys (skirts, longer hair), and for the men to do more masculine work (nursing men patients, becoming administrators).

The gendered social order constructs not only differences but gender inequality. Appropriate gender behavior builds up masculine dominance and feminine submissiveness. The gendered structure of family work puts more of the burden of housework and childcare on the wife, even if she is a high earner in a prestigious career. The gendered division of the labor market reserves better paying jobs and positions of authority for men. All this has been well documented by earlier feminisms. What social construction feminism reveals is how we all collude in maintaining the unequal gendered social order, most of the time without even realizing we are "doing gender."

Suggested Readings in Social Construction Feminism

Bem, Sandra Lipsitz. 1993. *The Lenses of Gender.* New Haven, CT: Yale University Press.

Berk, Sarah Fenstermaker. 1985. *The Gender Factory: The Apportionment of Work in American Households.* New York: Plenum.

Connell, R. W. 1987. *Gender and Power.* Stanford, CA: Stanford University Press.

DeVault, Marjorie L. 1991. *Feeding the Family: The Social Organization of Caring as Gender Work.* Chicago: University of Chicago Press.

Foucault, Michel. 1978. *The History of Sexuality: An Introduction.* (Trans. by Robert Hurley). New York: Pantheon.

Greenberg, David F. 1988. *The Construction of Homosexuality.* Chicago: University of Chicago Press.

Kessler, Suzanne J., and Wendy McKenna. 1978. *Gender: An Ethnomethodological Approach.* Chicago: University of Chicago Press.

Kitzinger, Celia. 1987. *The Social Construction of Lesbianism.* Newbury Park, CA: Sage.

Laqueur, Thomas. 1990. *Making Sex: Body and Gender from the Greeks to Freud.* Cambridge, MA: Harvard University Press.

Lorber, Judith. 1994. *Paradoxes of Gender.* New Haven, CT: Yale University Press.

Potuchek, Jean L. 1997. *Who Supports the Family? Gender and Breadwinning in Dual-Earner Marriages.* Stanford, CA: Stanford University Press.

Richardson, Diane (ed.). 1996. *Theorizing Heterosexuality: Telling It Straight.* Buckingham, Gt. Britain: Open University Press.

Risman, Barbara. 1997. *Gender Vertigo: Toward a Post-Gender Family.* New Haven, CT: Yale University Press.

Thorne, Barrie. 1993. *Gender Play: Girls and Boys at School.* New Brunswick, NJ: Rutgers University Press.

Chapter Eleven

Postmodern Feminism and Queer Theory

Sources of Gender Inequality

- The binary division of the social world into privileged and unprivileged gender and sexual categories
- The reproduction of these categories in cultural productions

Remedies

- Deliberately blurring gender and sexual boundaries
- Constant questioning of what is normal
- Popular culture that creates "queer" bodies, sexualities, and genders

Contributions

- Making visible the gender and sexual symbolism in mass culture that supports beliefs about what is normal and natural
- Making a place for homosexuality, bisexuality, transvestism, and transsexuality to be openly part of Western culture

Postmodern feminism and queer theory go the furthest in challenging gender categories as dual, oppositional, and fixed. They argue that sexuality and gender are shifting, fluid, multiple categories. They criticize a politics based on a universal category, Woman, and present instead a more subversive view that undermines the solidity of a social order built on two sexes, two sexualities, and two genders. Equality will come, they say, when there are so many recognized sexes, sexualities, and genders that one cannot be played against the other.

Postmodern feminism questions what we think we know about gender, as shown by the following excerpt from a paper originally presented in 1984 at the German Association for American Studies in Berlin. The author is a political theorist at Howard University and a psychotherapist who writes on feminist theory.

POSTMODERNISM AND GENDER RELATIONS

Jane Flax

. . . The fundamental purpose of feminist theory is to analyze how we think, or do not think, or avoid thinking about gender. Obviously, then, to understand the goals of feminist theory we must consider its central subject—gender.

Here, however, we immediately plunge into a complicated and controversial morass. For among feminist theorists there is by no means consensus on such (apparently) elementary questions as: What is gender? How is it related to anatomical sexual differences? How are gender relations constituted and sustained (in one person's lifetime and, more generally, as a social experience over time)? How do gender relations relate to other sorts of social relations such as class or race? Do gender relations have a history (or many)? What causes gender relations to change over time? What are the relationships between gender relations, sexuality, and a sense of individual identity? What are the relationships between heterosexuality, homosexuality, and gender relations? Are there only two genders? What are the relationships between forms of male dominance and gender relations? Could/would gender relations wither away in egalitarian societies? Is there anything distinctively male or female in modes of thought and social relations? If there is, are these distinctions innate or socially constituted? Are gendered distinctions socially useful or necessary? If so, what are the consequences for the feminist goal of attaining gender justice?

Confronted with such a bewildering set of questions, it is easy to overlook the fact that a fundamental transformation in social theory has occurred. The single most important advance in feminist theory is that the existence of gender relations has been problematized. Gender can no longer be treated as a simple, natural fact. The assumption that gender relations are natural arose from two coinciding circumstances: the unexamined identification and confusion of (anatomical) sexual differences with gender relations, and the absence of active feminist movements. . . .

Contemporary feminist movements are in part rooted in transformations in social experience that challenge widely shared categories of social meaning and explanation. In the United States, such transformations include changes in the structure of the economy, the family, the place of the United States in the world system, the declining authority of previously powerful social institutions, and the emergence of political groups that have increasingly more divergent ideas and demands concerning justice, equality, social legislation, and the proper role of the state. In such a decentered and unstable universe it seems plausible to question one of the most natural facets of human existence—gender relations. . . .

"Gender relations" is a category meant to capture a complex set of social processes. Gender, both as an analytic category and a social process, is relational. That is, gender relations are complex and unstable processes (or temporary totalities in the language of dialectics) constituted by and through interrelated parts. These parts are interdependent, that is, each part can have no meaning or existence without the others.

Gender relations are differentiated and (so far) asymmetric divisions and attributions of human traits and capacities. Through gender relations two types of persons are created: man and woman. Man and woman are posited as exclusionary categories. One can be only one gender, never the other or both. The actual content of being a man or woman and the rigidity of the categories themselves are highly variable across cultures and time. Nevertheless, gender relations so far as we have been able to understand them have been (more or less) relations of domination. That is, gender relations have been (more) defined and (imperfectly) controlled by one of their interrelated aspects—the man.

These relations of domination and the existence of gender relations themselves have been concealed in a variety of ways, including defining women as a "question" or the "sex" or the "other" and men as the universal (or at least without gender). In a wide variety of cultures and discourses, men tend to be seen as free from or as not determined by gender relations. Thus, for example, academics do not explicitly study the psychology of men or men's history. Male academics do not worry about how being men may distort their intellectual work, while women who study gender relations are considered suspect (of triviality, if not bias). Only recently have scholars begun to consider the possibility that there may be at least three histories in every culture—his, hers, and ours. *His* and *ours* are generally assumed to be equivalents, although in contemporary work there might be some recognition of the existence of that deviant—woman (e.g., women's history). However, it is still rare for scholars to search for the pervasive effects of gender relations on all aspects of a culture in the way that they feel obligated to investigate the impact of relations of power or the organization of production.

To the extent that feminist discourse defines its problematic as "woman," it, too, ironically privileges the man as unproblematic or exempted from determination by gender relations. From the perspective of social relations, men and women are both prisoners of gender, although in highly differentiated but interrelated ways. That men appear to be and (in many cases) are the wardens, or at least the trustees within a social whole, should not blind us to the extent to which they, too, are governed by the rules of gender. (This is not to deny that it matters a great deal—to individual men, to the women and children sometimes connected to them and to those concerned about justice—where men as well as women are distributed within social hierarchies.) . . .

One important barrier to our comprehension of gender relations has been the difficulty of understanding the relationship between *gender* and *sex*. In this context, *sex* means the anatomical differences between male and female. Historically (at least since Aristotle), these anatomical differences have been assigned to the class of natural facts or biology. In turn, biology has been equated with the pre- or nonsocial. Gender relations then become conceptualized as if they are constituted by two opposite terms or distinct types of being—man and woman. Since man and woman seem to be opposites or fundamentally distinct types of being, gender cannot be relational. If gender is as natural and as intrinsically a part of us as the genitals we are born with, it follows that it would be foolish (or even harmful) to attempt either to change gender arrangements or not to take them into account as a delimitation on human activities.

Even though a major focus of feminist theory has been to denaturalize gender, feminists as well as nonfeminists seem to have trouble thinking through the meanings we assign to and the uses we make of the concept "natural." What, after all, is the natural in the context of the human world? There are many aspects of our embodiedness or biology that we might see as given limits to human action which Western medicine and science do not hesitate to challenge. . . .

Thus, in order to understand gender as a social relation, feminist theorists need to deconstruct further the meanings we attach to biology/sex/gender/nature. This process of deconstruction is far from complete and certainly is not easy. Initially, some feminists thought we could merely separate the terms *sex* and *gender.* As we became more sensitive to the social histories of concepts, it became clear that such an (apparent) disjunction, while politically necessary, rested upon problematic and culture-specific oppositions, for example, the one between nature and culture or body and mind. As some feminists began to rethink these oppositions, new questions emerged: Does anatomy (body) have no relation to mind? What difference does it make in the constitution of my social experiences that I have a specifically female body?

Despite the increasing complexity of our questions, most feminists would still insist that gender relations are not (or are not only) equivalent to or a consequence of anatomy. Everyone will agree that there are anatomical differences between men and women. These anatomical differences seem to be primarily located in or are the consequence of the differentiated contributions men and woman make to a common biological necessity—the physical reproduction of our species.

However, the mere existence of such anatomical differentiation is a descriptive fact, one of many observations we might make about the physical characteristics of humans. Part of the problem in deconstruction of the meaning of biology/sex/gender/nature is that sex/gender has been one of the few areas in which (usually female) embodiment can be discussed at all in (nonscientific) Western discourses. There are many other aspects of our embodiedness that seem equally remarkable and interesting, for example, the incredible complexity of the structure and functioning of our brains, the extreme and relatively prolonged physical helplessness of the human neonate as compared to that of other (even related) species, or the fact that every one of us will die.

It is also the case that physically male and female humans resemble each other in many more ways than we differ. Our similarities are even more striking if we compare humans to, say, toads or trees. So why ought the anatomical differences between male and female humans assume such significance in our sense of ourselves as persons? Why ought such complex human social meanings and structures be based on or justified by a relatively narrow range of anatomical differences?

One possible answer to these questions is that the anatomical differences between males and females are connected to and are partially a consequence of one of the most important functions of the species—its physical reproduction. Thus, we might argue, because reproduction is such an important aspect of our species life, characteristics associated with it will be much more salient to us than, say, hair color or height.

Another possible answer to these questions might be that in order for humans physically to reproduce the species, we have to have sexual intercourse. Our anatomical differences make possible (and necessary for physical reproduction) a certain fitting together of distinctively male and female organs. For some humans this "fitting together" is also highly desirable and pleasurable. Hence, our anatomical differences seem to be inextricably connected to (and in some sense even causative of) sexuality.

Thus, there seems to be a complex of relations that have associated, given meanings: penis or clitoris, vagina, and breasts (read distinctively male or female bodies), sexuality (read reproduction—birth and babies), sense of self as a distinct, differentiated gender—as either (and only) male or female person (read gender relations as a natural exclusionary category). That is, we believe there are only two types of humans, and each of us can be only one of them.

A problem with all these apparently obvious associations is that they may assume precisely what requires explanation—that is, gender relations. We live in a world in which gender is a constituting social relation and in which gender is also a relation of domination. Therefore, both men's and women's understanding of anatomy, biology, embodiedness, sexuality, and reproduction is partially rooted in, reflects, and must justify (or challenge) preexisting gender relations. In turn, the existence of gender relations helps us to order and understand the facts of human existence. In other words, gender can become a metaphor for biology just as biology can become a metaphor for gender.

Prisoners of Gender

The apparent connections between gender relations and such important aspects of human existence as birth, reproduction, and sexuality make possible both a conflating of the natural and the social and an overly radical distinction between the two. In modern Western culture and sometimes even in feminist theories, the words *natural* and *social* become conflated in our understanding of "woman." In nonfeminist and some feminist writings about women, a radical disjunction is frequently made between the natural and the social. Women often stand for/symbolize the body, "difference," the concrete. These qualities are also said by some feminist as well as nonfeminist writers to suffuse/define the activities most associated with women: nurturing, mothering, taking care of and being in relation with others, preserving. Women's minds are also often seen as reflecting the qualities of our stereotypically female activities and bodies. Even feminists sometimes say women reason and write differently and have different interests and motives than men. Men are said to have more interest in utilizing the power of abstract reason (mind), to want mastery over nature (including bodies), and to be aggressive and militaristic.

The reemergence of such claims even among some feminists needs further analysis. Is this the beginning of a genuine transvaluation of values or a retreat into traditional gendered ways of understanding the world? In our attempts to correct arbitrary (and gendered) distinctions, feminists often end up reproducing them. Feminist discourse is full of contradictory and irreconcilable conceptions of the nature of our social relations, of men and women and the worth and character of stereotypically masculine and feminine activities. The positing of these conceptions such that only one perspective can be correct (or properly feminist) reveals, among other things, the embeddedness of feminist theory in the very social processes we are trying to critique and our need for more systematic and self-conscious theoretical practice. . . .

The enterprise of feminist theory is fraught with temptations and pitfalls. Insofar as women have been part of all societies, our thinking cannot be free from culture-bound modes of self-understanding. We as well as men internalize the dominant gender's conceptions of masculinity and femininity. Unless we see gender as a social relation rather than as an opposition of inherently different beings, we will not be able to identify the varieties and limitations of different women's (or men's) powers and oppressions within particular societies. Feminist theorists are faced with a fourfold task. We need to (1) articulate feminist viewpoints of/within the social worlds in which we live; (2) think about how we are affected by these worlds; (3) consider the ways in which how we think about them may be implicated in existing power/knowledge relationships; and (4) imagine ways in which these worlds ought to and can be transformed.

Since within contemporary Western societies gender relations have been ones of domination, feminist theories should have a compensatory as well as a critical aspect. That is, we need to recover and explore the aspects of social relations that have been suppressed, unarticulated, or denied within dominant (male) viewpoints. We need to recover and write the histories of women and our activities into the accounts and stories that cultures tell about themselves. Yet, we also need to think about how so-called women's activities are partially constituted by and through their location within the web of social relations that make up any society. That is, we need to know how these activities are affected but also how they effect, enable, or compensate for the consequences of men's activities, as well as their implication in class or race relations.

There should also be a transvaluation of values—a rethinking of our ideas about what is humanly excellent, worthy of praise, or moral. In such a transvaluation, we need to be careful not to assert merely the superiority of the opposite. For example, sometimes feminist theorists tend to oppose autonomy to being-in-relations. Such an opposition does not account for adult forms of being-in-relations that can be claustrophobic without autonomy—an autonomy that, without being-in-relations can easily degenerate into mastery. Our upbringing as women in this culture often encourages us to deny the many subtle forms of aggression that intimate relations with others can evoke and entail. For example, much of the discussion of mothering and the distinctively female tends to avoid discussing women's anger and aggression—how we internalize them and express them, for example, in relation to children or our own internal selves. Perhaps women are not any less aggressive than men; we may just express our aggression in different, culturally sanctioned (and partially disguised or denied) ways.

Since we live in a society in which men have more power than women, it makes sense to assume that what is considered to be more worthy of praise may be those qualities associated with men. As feminists, we have the right to suspect that even praise of the female may be (at least in part) motivated by a wish to keep women in a restricted (and restrictive) place. Indeed, we need to search into all aspects of a society (the feminist critique included) for the expressions and consequences of relations of domination. We should insist that all such relations are social, that is, they are not the result of the differentiated possession of natural and unequal properties among types of persons.

However, in insisting upon the existence and power of such relations of domination, we should avoid seeing women/ourselves as totally innocent, passive beings. Such a view prevents us from seeing the areas of life in which women have had an effect, in which we are less determined by the will of the other(s), and in which some of us have and do exert power over others (e.g., the differential privileges of race, class, sexual preference, age, or location in the world system).

Any feminist standpoint will necessarily be partial. Thinking about women may illuminate some aspects of a society that have been previously suppressed within the dominant view. But none of us can speak for "woman" because no such person exists except within a specific set of (already gendered) relations—to "man" and to many concrete and different women. . . .

Feminist theories, like other forms of postmodernism, should encourage us to tolerate and interpret ambivalence, ambiguity, and multiplicity as well as to expose the roots of our needs for imposing order and structure no matter how arbitrary and oppressive these needs may be.

If we do our work well, reality will appear even more unstable, complex, and disorderly than it does now. In this sense, perhaps Freud was right when he declared that women are the enemies of civilization.

Postmodern feminism and queer theory examine the ways societies create beliefs about gender at any time (now and in the past) with "discourses" embedded in cultural representations or "texts." Not just art, literature, and the mass media, but anything produced by a social group, including newspapers, political pronouncements, and religious liturgy, is a "text." A text's "discourse" is what it says, does not say, and hints at (sometimes called a "subtext"). The historical and social context and the material conditions under which a text is produced become part of the text's discourse. If a movie or newspaper is produced in a time of conservative values or under a repressive political regime, its "discourse" is going to be different from what is produced during times of openness or social change. Who provides the money, who does the creative work, and who oversees the managerial side all influence what a text conveys to its audience. The projected audience also shapes any text, although the actual audience may read quite different meanings from those intended by the producers. "Deconstruction" is the process of teasing out all these aspects of a "text."

The concepts of deconstruction and texts derived from cultural studies may sound quite esoteric, but we are all familiar with these processes. The coverage of Princess Diana's death and funeral created discourses about her—as wife, mother, divorcée, and benefactor. The days before the funeral were full of discourses on the meaning of royalty. Her funeral became a public ritual with a subtext on the proper expression of grief. As spectators, we read ourselves into the text of her life, using parallels with our own lives or fantasies about how we would like to live.

Soap operas and romance novels are "read" by women the way Diana's life was; action films and war novels are the stuff of men's spectatorship. Postmodern feminism deconstructs cultural representations of gender, as seen in movies, videos, TV, popular music, advertising—whether aimed at adults, teenagers, or children—as well as paintings, operas, theater productions, and ballet. All these media have discourses that overtly and subliminally tell us something about female and male bodies, sexual desire, and gender roles. A romantic song about the man who got away glorifies heterosexuality; a tragedy deploring the death of a salesman tells us that men's hard work should pay off. These discourses influence the way we think about our world, without questioning the underlying assumptions about gender and sexuality. They encourage approved-of choices about work, marriage, and having children by showing them as normal and rewarding and by showing what is disapproved of as leading to a "bad end." By unpacking texts of their covert as well as more obvious meanings, postmodern deconstruction reveals their messages. We can then accept or reject them, or use them for our own purposes.

Queer theory goes beyond cultural productions to examine the discourses of gender and sexuality in everyday life. In queer theory, gender and sexuality are "performances"—identities or selves we create as we display ourselves to others. What we wear and how we use our bodies are signs of gender and sexual orientation. Gender and sexuality can be masked, parodied, flaunted, played with, and mixed up any way we want. Recently, in the audience at an academic lecture was a young man with a conventional haircut but with orange hair, one long earring, lipstick, blue nail polish on fingers and toes, a unisex black T-shirt, a yellow sarong skirt of the kind worn by men and women in tropical resorts, and clunky open-toed sandals. Queer theorists have explored whether such mixed gender displays create a freer social space.

Cross-dressing for "drag" performances, costume parties, Mardi Gras, and gay pride parades are displays of queerness, deliberately playing with gender and sexuality. But when a male transvestite or transsexual wants to be "read" as woman, he wears a demure dress, stockings, and high-heeled shoes. Someone whose looks are unconventionally gendered and who does not want to be forced to conform is in a painfully ambiguous status. The lady with a beard is stared at openly on the street and can find work only in a circus.

Is the circus, night club, or theater the only place gender can be defied? Or can we be gender rebels or "queers" in everyday life? The following excerpt is by one of the chief proponents of queer theory. She is professor of English at Duke University and has written about ambiguities and "closets" in literature and in recent history. Here, she shows how normative social reality is created, and how questioning the linked binary components of gender and sexuality subverts, or queers, that reality.

What's Queer?

Eve Kosofsky Sedgwick

What's "queer"? Here's one train of thought about it. The depressing thing about the Christmas season—isn't it?—is that it's the time when all the institutions are speaking with one voice. The Church says what the Church says. But the State says the same thing: maybe not (in some ways it hardly matters) in the language of theology, but in the language the State talks: legal holidays, long school hiatus, special postage stamps, and all. And the language of commerce more than chimes in, as consumer purchasing is organized ever more narrowly around the final weeks of the calendar year, the Dow Jones aquiver over Americans' "holiday mood." The media, in turn, fall in triumphally behind the Christmas phalanx: ad-swollen magazines have oozing turkeys on the cover, while for the news industry every question turns into the Christmas question—Will hostages be free *for Christmas?* What did that flash flood or mass murder (umpty-ump people killed and maimed) do to those families' *Christmas?* And meanwhile, the pairing "families/Christmas" becomes increasingly tautological, as families more and more constitute themselves according to the schedule, and in the endlessly iterated image, of the holiday itself constituted in the image of "the" family.

The thing hasn't, finally, so much to do with propaganda for Christianity as with propaganda for Christmas itself. They all—religion, state, capital, ideology, domesticity, the discourses of power and legitimacy—line up with each other so neatly once a year, and the monolith so created is a thing one can come to view with unhappy eyes. What if instead there were a practice of valuing the ways in which meanings and institutions can be at loose ends with each other? What if the richest junctures weren't the ones where *everything means the same thing?* Think of that entity "the family," an impacted social space in which all of the following are meant to line up perfectly with each other:

a surname

a sexual dyad

a legal unit based on state-regulated marriage

a circuit of blood relationships

a system of companionship and succor

a building

a proscenium between "private" and "public"

an economic unit of earning and taxation

the prime site of economic consumption

the prime site of cultural consumption

a mechanism to produce, care for, and acculturate children

a mechanism for accumulating material goods over several generations

a daily routine

a unit in a community of worship

a site of patriotic formation

and of course the list could go on. Looking at my own life, I see that—probably like most people—I have valued and pursued these various elements of family identity to quite differing degrees (e.g., no use at all for worship, much need of companionship). But what's been consistent in this particular life is an interest in not letting very many of these dimensions line up directly with each other at one time. I see it's been a ruling intuition for me that the most productive strategy (intellectually, emotionally) might be, whenever possible, to *dis*articulate them one from another, to *dis*engage them—the bonds of blood, of law, of habitation, of privacy, of companionship and succor—from the lockstep of their unanimity in the system called "family."

Or think of all the elements that are condensed in the notion of sexual identity, something that the common sense of our time presents as a unitary category. Yet, exerting any pressure at all on "sexual identity," you see that its elements include

your biological (e.g., chromosomal) sex, male or female;

your self-perceived gender assignment, male or female (supposed to be the same as your biological sex);

the preponderance of your traits of personality and appearance, masculine or feminine (supposed to correspond to your sex and gender);

the biological sex of your preferred partner;

the gender assignment of your preferred partner (supposed to be the same as her/his biological sex);

the masculinity or femininity of your preferred partner (supposed to be the opposite* of your own);

your self-perception as gay or straight (supposed to correspond to whether your preferred partner is your sex or the opposite);

your preferred partner's self-perception as gay or straight (supposed to be the same as yours);

your procreative choice (supposed to be yes if straight, no if gay);

your preferred sexual act(s) (supposed to be insertive if you are male or masculine, receptive if you are female or feminine);

your most eroticized sexual organs (supposed to correspond to the procreative capabilities of your sex, and to your insertive/receptive assignment);

your sexual fantasies (supposed to be highly congruent with your sexual practice, but stronger in intensity);

your main locus of emotional bonds (supposed to reside in your preferred sexual partner);

your enjoyment of power in sexual relations (supposed to be low if you are female or feminine, high if male or masculine);

the people from whom you learn about your own gender and sex (supposed to correspond to yourself in both respects);

your community of cultural and political identification (supposed to correspond to your own identity);

* The binary calculus I'm describing here depends on the notion that the male and female sexes are each other's "opposites," but I do want to register a specific demurral against that bit of easy common sense. Under no matter what cultural construction, women and men are more like each other than chalk is like cheese, than ratiocination is like raisins, than up is like down, or than 1 is like 0. The biological, psychological, and cognitive attributes of men overlap with those of women by vastly more than they differ from them.

and—again—many more. Even this list is remarkable for the silent presumptions it has to make about a given person's sexuality, presumptions that are true only to varying degrees, and for many people not true at all: that everyone "has a sexuality," for instance, and that it is implicated with each person's sense of overall identity in similar ways; that each person's most characteristic erotic expression will be oriented toward another person and not autoerotic; that if it is alloerotic, it will be oriented toward a single partner or kind of partner at a time; that its orientation will not change over time. Normatively, as the parenthetical prescriptions in the list above suggest, it should be possible to deduce anybody's entire set of specs from the initial datum of biological sex alone—if one adds only the normative assumption that "the biological sex of your preferred partner" will be the opposite of one's own. With or without that heterosexist assumption, though, what's striking is the number and *differ-*

ence of the dimensions that "sexual identity" is supposed to organize into a seamless and univocal whole.

And if it doesn't?

That's one of the things that "queer" can refer to: the open mesh of possibilities, gaps, overlaps, dissonances and resonances, lapses and excesses of meaning when the constituent elements of anyone's gender, of anyone's sexuality aren't made (or *can't be* made) to signify monolithically. The experimental linguistic, epistemological, representational, political adventures attaching to the very many of us who may at times be moved to describe ourselves as (among many other possibilities) pushy femmes, radical faeries, fantasists, drags, clones, leatherfolk, ladies in tuxedoes, feminist women or feminist men, masturbators, bulldaggers, divas, Snap! queens, butch bottoms, storytellers, transsexuals, aunties, wannabes, lesbian-identified men or lesbians who sleep with men, or . . . people able to relish, learn from, or identify with such.

Again, "queer" can mean something different: a lot of the way I have used it so far in this dossier is to denote, almost simply, same-sex sexual object choice, lesbian or gay, whether or not it is organized around multiple criss-crossings of definitional lines. And given the historical and contemporary force of the prohibitions against *every* same-sex sexual expression, for anyone to disavow those meanings, or to displace them from the term's definitional center, would be to dematerialize any possibility of queerness itself.

At the same time, a lot of the most exciting recent work around "queer" spins the term outward along dimensions that can't be subsumed under gender and sexuality at all: the ways that race, ethnicity, postcolonial nationality crisscross with these *and other* identity-constituting, identity-fracturing discourses, for example. Intellectuals and artists of color whose sexual self-definition includes "queer"—I think of an Isaac Julien, a Gloria Anzaldúa, a Richard Fung—are using the leverage of "queer" to do a new kind of justice to the fractal intricacies of language, skin, migration, state. Thereby, the gravity (I mean the *gravitas*, the meaning, but also the *center* of gravity) of the term "queer" itself deepens and shifts. . . .

Critique. If social construction feminism puts too much emphasis on institutions and structures and not enough on individual actions, postmodern feminism and queer theory have just the opposite problem.

In queer theory, all the emphasis is on agency, impression management, and presentation of the self in the guise and costume most likely to produce or parody conformity. Postmodern feminism is mainly concerned with deconstructing cultural productions, neglecting the more iron-bound and controlling discourses embedded in organizational, legal, religious, and political texts.

Social construction feminism's analyses of the institutional and organizational practices that maintain the gender order could be combined with postmodern feminist and queer theory's deconstruction of how individuals do and undo gender. Social construction feminism argues that the gendered social order is constantly restabilized by individual action, but queer theory has shown how individuals can consciously and purposefully create disorder and gender instability, opening the way to social change.

Summary

Postmodern feminism and queer theory question all the conventional assumptions about gender and sexuality, arguing that the categories of "man," "woman," "heterosexual," "homosexual," "male," "female," are performances and displays. Like social construction feminism, postmodern feminism claims that gender is created in the doing—the way we dress, use our bodies, talk, behave. But postmodern feminists do not focus on the social structures that are built up out of repeated gender performances. They argue that gender and sexuality are always in flux, never fixed. There are no permanent identities, making identity politics questionable.

Politically, postmodern feminists are interested in deconstructing the messages we get about gender and sexuality in the mass media, popular culture, and the arts. These messages or "texts" are subliminal sermons on how to be a man, a woman, and how each should be heterosexually sexy. If we can see through these messages, we can, if we want, reject or modify them.

Queer theory advocates going even further in destabilizing gender and sexuality. Queer theorists parody and play with gender and sexuality. A drag queen, who parodies femininity, and Marilyn Monroe and Madonna, who exaggerate their sexuality, are equally queer examples of female impersonators. Queer politics disturbs what we think is normal and natural. In queer theory, a body can be female and male at the same time, as when a preoperative transsexual uses hormones to grow breasts but still has a penis. Bisexuality upsets the heterosexual–homosexual division. And genders can be as numerous as the imagination can dream up.

Postmodern feminism and queer theory are playful but have the serious intent of making us think about what we take for granted—that men and women, homosexuals and heterosexuals, males and females are totally different creatures, and that we can't make and remake ourselves.

Suggested Readings in Postmodern Feminism and Queer Theory

Bornstein, Kate. 1994. *Gender Outlaw: On Men, Women, and the Rest of Us.* New York: Vintage.

Butler, Judith. 1990. *Gender Trouble: Feminism and the Subversion of Identity.* New York and London: Routledge.

——. 1993. *Bodies that Matter: On the Discursive Limits of "Sex."* New York and London: Routledge.

DeLauretis, Teresa. 1984. *Alice Doesn't: Feminism, Semiotics, Cinema.* Bloomington: Indiana University Press.

Epstein, Julia, and Kristina Straub. 1991. *Body Guards: The Cultural Politics of Gender Ambiguity.* New York and London: Routledge.

Garber, Marjorie. 1992. *Vested Interests: Cross-Dressing and Cultural Anxiety.* New York and London: Routledge.

——. 1995. *Vice Versa: Bisexuality and the Eroticism of Everyday Life.* New York: Simon and Schuster.

Herdt, Gilbert (ed.). 1994. *Third Sex, Third Gender: Beyond Sexual Dimorphism in Culture and History.* New York: Zone Books.

Kates, Gary. 1995. *Monsieur d'Eon Is a Woman: A Tale of Political Intrigue and Sexual Masquerade.* New York: Basic Books.

Nicholson, Linda J. (ed.). 1990. *Feminism/Postmodernism.* New York and London: Routledge.

Sedgwick, Eve Kosofsky. 1990. *Epistemology of the Closet.* Berkeley: University of California Press.

——. 1993. *Tendencies.* Durham, NC: Duke University Press.

Walters, Suzanna Danuta. 1995. *Material Girls: Making Sense of Feminist Cultural Theory.* Berkeley: University of California Press.

Warner, Michael (ed.). 1993. *Fear of a Queer Planet: Queer Politics and Social Theory.* Ann Arbor: University of Michigan Press.

Woodhouse, Annie. 1989. *Fantastic Women: Sex, Gender, and Transvestism.* New Brunswick, NJ: Rutgers University Press.

Part V

Feminism's Future Work: A Personal Viewpoint

As a social constructionist, I think that if feminism is going to have a significant impact on the pervasive gendering of the social order, it has to focus on gender as a social status for individuals and as one of the main building blocks of society. It has to show clearly how social processes, social relations, and social structures—not biology—construct gender. If the current unequal gendered social order in modern societies is seen as a human construction and not believed to be the inevitable product of hormones or genetic hard-wiring or prenatal brain structuring, then we have a real chance to change it.

In this section, I will discuss how we can think about deconstructing gender, and how social practices can be structured for gender equality.[1]

(De)Constructing Difference

Most societies carefully create differences between boys and girls and women and men and patrol the boundaries between them with the powers of the state and the pressures of everyday interaction (Gerson and Peiss 1985). Maintaining gender differences through social practices is essential to the ranking of the women of each social group below the men of that group and to the legitimation of the economic, emotional, and sexual exploitation of women. The conventional gendered identities and normative expectations for women and men are legitimized and reinforced by cultural productions and sports, the mass media, science, religion, and other value-laden "discourses." In short, societies construct gender differences and then justify different treatment of women and men on the basis of those socially constructed differences.

To undermine this social construction, some feminists have tried to show that men and women are not that different. That tactic has not been very successful because so many people believe that because of biology, women and men *are* very different. Race and ethnicity are clearly socially constructed groupings, but most people assume that sex, sexuality, and gender are self-evident and "natural." They are socially constructed as well.

Beyond Binaries

Human beings are a mix of many attributes and characteristics, but only a few of these are life-long markers of social identity. In order to be able to put people into a few categories, differences among them are ignored. Sex, sexuality, and gender are socially constructed to be binary—to have two and only two possibilities—but there are actually multiple sexes, sexualities, and genders.[2]

Sex

Every man produces estrogen and every woman produces testosterone, so hormonally, we are not so easily split into "opposite sexes" (Angier 1994, 1995). An anomaly common enough to be found at every major international sports competition is the existence of XY chromosomes in female athletes who do not have male genitalia or physiology because of other genetic input, so chromosomes cannot be used as an indicator of female sex (Grady 1992). Physiologically, there is overlap in females' and males' muscular strength and physical endurance that is ignored in the rules for women's competitions (Kane 1995).

This mixture of genes, hormones, and physiology produces bodies that on crude inspection can be classified as "male" or "female." But significant ambiguities occur fairly often. Male and female genitalia develop from the same fetal tissue; because of various genetic and hormonal inputs, at least 1 in 1000 infants are born with ambiguous genitalia, and perhaps more (Fausto-Sterling 1993). These incongruences are hidden or altered surgically and hormonally. The alterations are justified by the difficulties of raising a sexually ambiguous child, and by projected psychological problems for the child. They are usually not medically necessary (Angier 1997, Cowley 1997).

Suzanne Kessler (1990) interviewed six medical specialists in pediatric intersexuality and found that an infant with XY chromosomes, a very small penis, and an incompletely closed scrotum is usually categorized as a girl, despite male chromosomes, and sex-change surgery is used to make a clitoris out of the penis and a vagina out of the scrotum. Medical opinion is that a boy with a very small penis would be severely handicapped. Even though it is very difficult to do surgery on newborns, doctors feel that parents cannot live with babies that have genitalia that are not clearly female or male. Newborns must be put into a sex category at birth. We have no "Baby X's."[3]

Sexuality

Studies of sexuality have shown that the conventional two-fold sexual categories are hard to document empirically (Klein et al. 1985, Weinberg et al. 1994, Wishik 1996). A sexual identity or orientation involves desired and actual sexual attraction and fantasies, not just behavior. It also includes emotional preferences, social preferences, and self-identification. All sexual identities and orientations—heterosexual, homosexual, bisexual, transsexual, transvestite—are responses not just to an individual's psyche but also to social pressures from family and friends. Because Western culture constructs sexuality dichotomously, many people whose sexual experiences are bisexual are forced to choose between a heterosexual and homosexual identity as their "real" identity (Rust 1993).

These social pressures suppress the sexual ambiguities and mixes and changes over time that are common in many people's lives, including the famous lover, Casanova. According to his memoirs, Casanova, a notorious seducer of women, liked his lovers to dress him up as a girl (Smith 1997). Although he preferred women, he also had homosexual experiences.

Gender

We know that gender is cross-cut by race, ethnicity, and social class, to give us many kinds of women and men. Resisting a global grouping of women and men that renders class and race differences invisible, feminists with a racial ethnic and class perspective have forced a reconsideration of stereotypes of "us" and "them" (Collins 1990; Trinh 1989). They have also laid out how inextricably linked race, class, and gender are and revealed their pervasive structural effects. The combinations of social characteristics are not just added to each other; each affects the others, and they work with or against each other. Thus, a Black woman surgeon has two "negative" and one "positive" status.

Although race and gender are both powerful status markers, in many societies it is illegal to classify people on the basis of their race, but it is not illegal to classify them by gender. In the United States, official papers, such as drivers' licenses, do not list a person's race, but they always list a person's gender.

Thus, the conventional dual or binary categories of female/male, homosexual/heterosexual, and woman/man are superimposed on a variety of behaviors, identifications, and feelings. Yet the categories we take for granted in our own society are not universal. There are non-Western societies that have third and fourth genders that link genitalia, sexual orientation, and gender status in ways quite different from Western cultures.

The Native American *berdache* is an institutionalized cross-gendered role in which males dress and work like women (Williams 1986). They marry men as wives, and they act as mother to adopted children. Berdaches' sex is male, and their sexuality is homosexual, but their gender status is not that of a man but of a woman. Two berdaches do not have sexual relations with each other, nor do they marry.

The Plains Indians had a tradition of *warrior women*. In that society and in other Native American societies that were egalitarian and tolerant of cross-gendered work activities, young women could live as men (Blackwood 1984, Whitehead 1981). Among the Mohave in the nineteenth century, a girl's refusal to learn women's tasks could lead to her being taught the same skills boys learned and to ritual renaming, nose piercing, and hair styling as a man. At that point, her status as a man allowed her to marry a woman and to do men's work of hunting, trapping, growing crops, and fighting. She was also expected to perform a man's ritual obligations. Because divorce was frequent and children went with the mother, a cross-gendered woman who married a woman with children could be a parent. Adoptions were also common. Sexually, cross-gendered women were homosexual, but, like berdaches, their marriages were always with a person of another gender—they did not marry or have sexual relationships with each other. In some African cultures today, a wealthy woman can marry a woman, thus acquiring a wife to do the woman's work; she adopts her wife's children as a father (Amadiume 1987).

In our society, we have two and only two genders. Gendered roles are built into all of the organizations and institutions that structure modern society, such as workplaces, governments, the military, religions, and the educational, legal, and health-care systems. These roles force us to be a man or a woman—with clearly differentiated behavior. They also set up expectations about physical competence, abilities, skills, motivations, and interests for women and men. These status expectations shape interaction and are an important mechanism in the preservation of gender inequality because men's attributes are considered superior to women's attributes (Ridgeway 1992).

When women enter formerly men-only organizations, or vice versa, a destabilizing effect of sometimes seismic proportions is set in motion. The first woman to be accepted at the all-male military academy, the Citadel, was taken for a man. There was no place on the application to check off M or F, since only men were supposed to apply. When a woman whose school performance and qualities were the equivalent of a man's was accepted, it showed the irrelevance of gender. That was the basis for the successful legal arguments for the admission of women.

However, when women were finally admitted and the school was degendered, a regendering process was quickly set in motion. All the first-year men get "knob" haircuts, or shaved heads, so they will look indistinguishable. The first-year women were told that they would get only very short haircuts. Wanting to be just like the men, they went off campus and got their heads shaved. They were punished for it. The photos published in the newspapers told the gender story very graphically: with shaved heads, you could not tell the girls from the boys. And that was just what the administrators of the Citadel did *not* want.

If the construction of the categories and the social processes of gender inequality are made visible (deconstructed), they might eventually be altered by individuals, groups, and whole societies. A social constructionist concept of gender assumes that because human beings have constructed and have used gender, human beings can deconstruct and stop using gender—and that would be *revolutionary*.

Structuring for Gender Equality

Destabilizing the carefully constructed gender categories that supply the rationale for treating all women as different from all men could undermine the two-genders social order. But a social order based on multiple genders is a long way off.

In the meantime, what can be done if we focus on gender inequality? Since gender is today a system of power and dominance mostly favoring men, redressing the imbalance would mean giving women some of men's privileges, such as freedom from housework, and giving men some of women's responsibilities, such as taking care of infants. Instead, men have received such women's privileges as limits on the number of hours a day a paid worker can be required to work, and women have received such men's responsibilities as economic support of their families. Lesbians and homosexual men are able to break the micro-system of domination and subordination, since personal power differentials are not genderered in their families and their communities. Nevertheless, they participate in the gendered macro-system, especially in the world of work, as women and men.

So how could we structure the family, workplace, and all other major institutions for equality?

Since race and class are intertwined with gender in the social arrangements that produce inequality, it is highly unlikely that gender inequality alone could (or should) be redressed without considering racial and economic exploitation. For example, capitalism currently exploits women as a reserve army of cheap labor, but it also exploits disadvantaged men. Profits are higher in any kind of economy if some workers are paid less than others, but these lesser-paid workers are not necessarily women. Economic systems do not need gendered job segregation or gendered occupational stratification to survive in their current forms; they need only low-cost workers and hierarchies of management. If the low-paid and high-paid workers were a random mix of women and men and if the owners and managers were also mixed in gender, equality of women and men in each stratum could be accomplished, but income inequalities and hierarchies of authority would still exist.

However, people with different social characteristics are rarely randomly sorted into a stratification system because social characteristics are used to create or justify the contingencies of inequality—the structure of the education system, the rewards for different kinds of work, the allocation of responsibility for the care of dependents. Any socially constructed categories can be used to stratify a society.

If we want to eliminate the exploitation of any social group by any other social group, a society has to be structured for equality.

That means that all individuals within a group and all social groups within a society have to be guaranteed equal access to the valued resources of the society—education; work; income for a comfortable standard of living; opportunities for satisfying emotional, sexual, and familial relationships; freedom from violence and exploitation; help in times of dependence; and the opportunity to produce knowledge, create culture, and lead in small and large ways.

In order for individuals to be equal, the social groups that order their lives (their families, work organizations, schools, religions, ethnicities, sexual communities) have to be structured for equality, and within those groups, all the members have to be social equals. That does not mean that they are all the same or even similar but that their diversity and separate contributions are equally valued and rewarded.

The meta-rule in a social order structured for equality is that no individual within a group and no group within the society monopolizes the economic, educational, and cultural resources, or the positions of power.

To make all workers equal, everyone who does any kind of socially useful work, including the caretakers of dependents, must receive an income that sustains a comfortable standard of living. Management that is shared or rotated could flatten hierarchies, so there would be no point for the members of any group to monopolize positions of authority.

If, after such a restructuring, some people, or some groups of people, disproportionately continued to be the caretakers of dependents, and if the production of goods and services continued to be more highly valued than bringing up children and taking care of the social and emotional needs of family members, inequality would persist. For true equality, care of children and the elderly would have to be made the equal responsibility of every able-bodied adult, perhaps in a vertical kinship system, with each competent adult responsible for a child and an elderly parent or grandparent (Lorber 1975). Some way of making caretakers economically independent has to be provided—if necessary, through government benefits.

Pregnancy and childbirth are not insurmountable barriers to structures of equality. Most modern women have two to three children at most. And if parenting is seen as many adults' responsibility, then social, emotional, and economic support during pregnancy and childbirth could certainly be given by those not pregnant or giving birth to the woman who gestates and delivers a child for the family or the household.

Structuring for equality would do away not with procreative differences but with social roles and patterns of behavior that assign responsibilities to all women that have nothing to do with pregnancy and childbirth. Many women are not and never will be birth mothers. Egalitarian childcare and child support are already structured into some dual-career and two-income families, joint custody arrangements, and gay and lesbian households.

If every adult in a household is to be equal, household income has to be shared equally; otherwise, the person with more economic resources has greater bargaining power. But a household of unequal earners can be structured for equality. All household income could be pooled and allocated first to food, clothing, shelter, transportation, medical care, school fees, and other household expenses (perhaps including paid childcare, house cleaning, laundry), donations, gifts, entertainment, vacations, retirement, and savings for emergencies. After that, to assure equal resources, the remainder could be split evenly among the adult members of the household for their individual use. Each adult in a household should be able to claim the same amount of discretionary income regardless of earnings, since that surplus buys the freedom to travel, donate, entertain, give gifts, save, work on private projects, and so on. Any earnings from this discretionary income should belong to the individual investor, who is risking her or his own money. Individuals should also be able to leave what they have accumulated to whomever they want.

All family work, including responsibility for hiring and overseeing paid helpers, would have to be evenly split or allocated by desirability, competence, convenience, and time. If all adults shared responsibility for domestic work, each would have equivalent time for educational and occupational advancement and political work. Any grouping of adults could live together, share both the income from paid work and their domestic labor and thus provide economic support and nurturing care for the children, elderly, and sick in a household. If the economic system and the political system were also structured for equality (by equitable income distribution and rotated positions of authority), the egalitarian structure of domestic life would support and be supported by the egalitarian structure of work and government.

Freed of exploitative economic, kinship, and procreative relationships, sexuality could indeed be the result of individual desires. But not all kinds of sexual behavior would be acceptable in an egalitarian society. Relations between adults and children and those imbued with acts of violence would erase the structural conditions of equality—that no one be exploited or subordinated in any way or by any means by anyone or any social institution. Children's equality depends on the protection of adults, protection that is violated by sexual exploitation. Violence creates the ultimate condition of inequality—unequal power—and so any use or threat of physical harm of one person by another must be absolutely forbidden legally, and tabooed culturally as well. But for socially competent adults, all consenting sexual relationships, including those with *fantasies* of violence, would have equal value in a society structured for equality.

Currently, the subordination, exploitation, and even extermination of some social groups by others as well as the inequality of individuals within all social groups is part of the government and criminal justice systems of most countries, even those supposedly organized for equality, such as the United States. If societies are to reverse this pattern of inequality and build on their traditional or constitutional structures of equality, at a minimum every proposed law, court order, or state policy must be examined first for its effect on all the structural conditions of equality: the distribution of economic resources, including services provided by the state; production of knowledge and culture; shares of political power; help for children, the elderly, the sick, the less physically and mentally competent; appreciation of ethnic traditions and religious beliefs; and acceptance of consenting adults' sexual practices.

Does a social world structured for equality mean people will be a varied, motley crew or a version of middle-class, White, Anglo-Saxon Protestant men? It would probably take a deliberate effort to counteract dominant masculine values in workplaces and other organizations, and to encourage diverse participation by all sorts of people. But if multiple sexes, sexualities, and genders, as well as multiple races, ethnic groups, and religions, become the social norm, then diversity and equality could also become the way of our world.

Summary

This brief review showed how the major social categories of sex, sexuality, and gender are constructed to be dual or binary by focusing on only a few characteristics. The characteristics of males, heterosexuals, and men are considered superior to those of females, homosexuals, and women. These categories, then, are built into a system of gender inequality. Together with other socially constructed categories, such as race and ethnicity, they build a social order that gives certain groups of people greater advantages, privileges, and opportunities to make a good life.

I argue that making the social construction of seemingly natural categories visible could lead to their deconstruction—their breakup into multiple categories of people. This multiplicity of groups has the potential to undermine the system of inequality that is built on a few identifiable and supposedly clearly different genders, sexes, sexualities, races, religions, and ethnic groups.

Such a disruption of the social order, especially with regard to gender, is unlikely to occur in the near future. Every time changes in gender patterns create an upheaval, as when women enter an organization formerly all men, people quickly restore gender distinctions by creating new ways to differentiate women from men. The persistence of single-user bathrooms carefully labeled "ladies" and "gents" is an example of gendering that we see every day.

A more practical goal for redressing gender inequality is to set up structures of work and family life that build in equality by distributing responsibilities and rewards absolutely even-handedly to people of diverse social characteristics doing different tasks. Parenting would be a job equal to breadwinning, and all adult members of a household would have equal economic resources. However, for true equality, workplaces would also have to be organized on the same principle of equal worth for a variety of jobs. Legal systems would have to be scrupulously examined for laws with an impact on inequality, and cultural productions would have to be reviewed for negative implications for any social group.

Much of what I describe as feminism's future work is already underway. But whether the focus is dismantling the categories on which the unequal gendered social order is built, or structuring for gender equality, there is a long way to go. One last caveat—perfect gender equality or a non-gendered world is not going to put the whole world right. The other social characteristics used to discriminate and disadvantage some members of a society have to be made irrelevant as well. However, instead of waiting for the whole world to be put right before we can have a feminist revolution, I would like to have the feminist revolution first—and then maybe the whole world will get put right that much faster.

Notes

1. Adapted from Lorber, Judith. 1994. *Paradoxes of Gender*. New Haven, CT: Yale University Press.
2. For a longer discussion, see Lorber 1996.
3. In 1972, *Ms. Magazine* published a fantasy of how to raise a child free of gender-typing. The experiment calls for hiding the child's anatomy from all eyes except the parents' and treating the child as neither a girl nor a boy. The child, called X, gets to do all the things boys *and* girls do. The experiment is so successful that all the children in X's class at school want to look and behave like X (Gould 1972).

References

Amadiume, Ifi. 1987. *Male Daughters, Female Husbands: Gender and Sex in an African Society*. London: Zed Books.

Angier, Natalie. 1994. "Male Hormone Molds Women, Too, in Mind and Body." *The New York Times*, May 3, C1, 13.

——. 1995. "Does Testosterone Equal Aggression? Maybe Not." *The New York Times*, June 20, A1, C3.

——. 1997. "New Debate Over Surgery on Genitals." *The New York Times*, May 13, C1, 6.

Blackwood, Evelyn. 1984. "Sexuality and Gender in Certain Native American Tribes: The Case of Cross-gender Females." *Signs* 10:27–42.

Collins, Patricia Hill. 1990. *Black Feminist Thought: Knowledge, Consciousness, and the Politics of Empowerment*. Boston: Unwin Hyman.

Cowley, Geoffrey. 1997. "Gender Limbo." *Newsweek*, May 19, 64–66.

Fausto-Sterling, Anne. 1993. "The Five Sexes: Why Male and Female Are Not Enough." *The Sciences*, March/April:20–25.

Gerson, Judith M., and Kathy Peiss. 1985. "Boundaries, Negotiation, Consciousness: Reconceptualizing Gender Relations." *Social Problems* 32:317–31.

Gould, Lois. 1972. "X: A Fabulous Child's Story." *Ms. Magazine*, (December): 74–76, 105–06.

Grady, Denise. 1992. "Sex Test of Champions: Olympic Officials Struggle to Define What Should Be Obvious: Just Who Is a Female Athlete." *Discover* 13(June):78–82.

Kane, Mary Jo. 1995. "Resistance/Transformation of the Oppositional Binary: Exposing Sport as a Continuum." *Journal of Sport and Social Issues* 19:213–40.

Kessler, Suzanne J. 1990. "The Medical Construction of Gender: Case Management of Intersexed Infants." *Signs* 16:3–26.

Klein, Fritz, Barry Sepekoff, and Timothy J. Wolf. 1985. "Sexual Orientation: A Multi-Variable Dynamic Process." *Journal of Homosexuality* 11(1/2):35–49.

Lorber, Judith. 1975. "Beyond Equality of the Sexes: The Question of the Children." *Family Coordinator* 24:465–72.

—. 1996. "Beyond the Binaries: Depolarizing the Categories of Sex, Sexuality, and Gender." *Sociological Inquiry* 66:143–59.

Ridgeway, Cecilia L. (ed.). 1992. *Gender, Interaction, and Inequality*. New York: Springer-Verlag.

Rust, Paula C. 1993. "'Coming out' in the Age of Social Constructionism: Sexual Identity Formation among Lesbian and Bisexual Women." *Gender & Society* 7:50–77.

Smith, Dinitia. 1997. "Learning to Love a Lover." *The New York Times*, October 1, E1, 4.

Trinh, T. Minh-ha. 1989. *Woman, Native, Other: Writing Postcoloniality and Feminism*. Bloomington: Indiana University Press.

Weinberg, Martin S., Colin J. Williams, and Douglas W. Pryor. 1994. *Dual Attraction: Understanding Bisexuality*. New York: Oxford University Press.

Whitehead, Harriet. 1981. "The Bow and the Burden Strap: A New Look at Institutionalized Homosexuality in Native North America." Pp. 80–115 in Sherry B. Ortner and Harriet Whitehead (eds). *Sexual Meanings: The Cultural Construction of Gender and Sexuality*. Cambridge, UK: Cambridge University Press.

Williams, Walter L. 1986. *The Spirit and the Flesh: Sexual Diversity in American Indian Culture*. Boston: Beacon.

Wishik, Heather R. 1996. "Life Maps: Tracking Individual Gender and Sexual Identity Construction in the Contexts of Cultures, Relationships, and Desires." *Journal of Gay, Lesbian, and Bisexual Identity* 1:129–52.